EYEWITNESS
SHARK

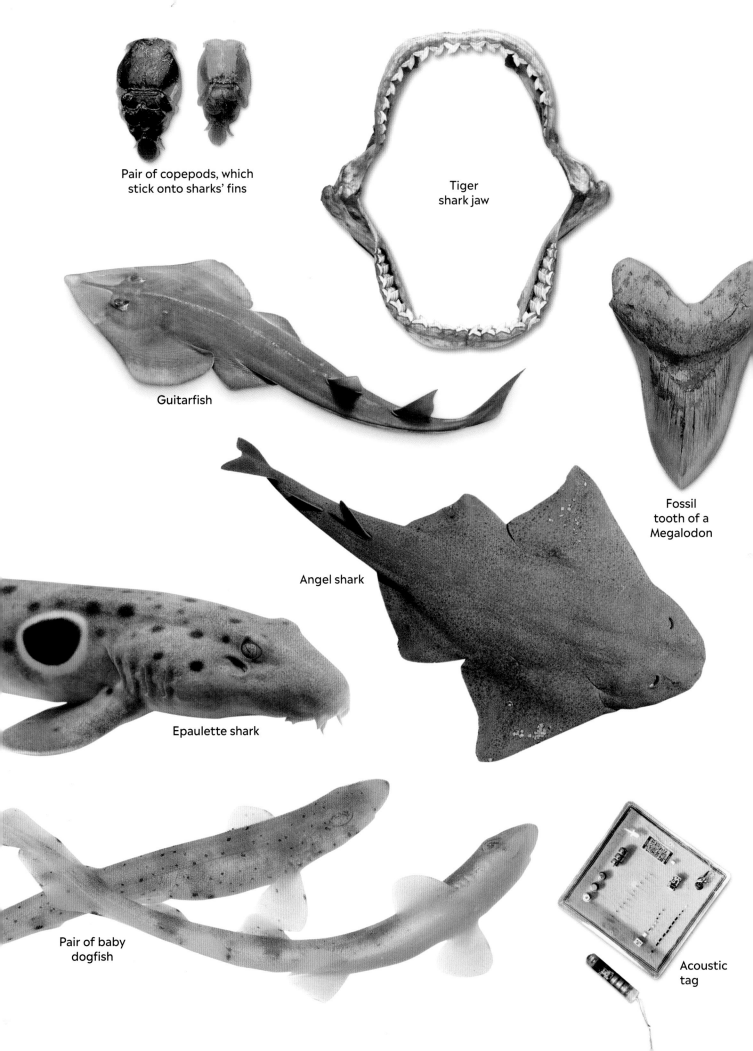

Pair of copepods, which stick onto sharks' fins

Tiger shark jaw

Guitarfish

Fossil tooth of a Megalodon

Angel shark

Epaulette shark

Pair of baby dogfish

Acoustic tag

E Y E W I T N E S S

SHARK

WRITTEN BY
MIRANDA MACQUITTY

Model of a male
great white shark

REVISED EDITION

Pair of starry
smooth-hounds

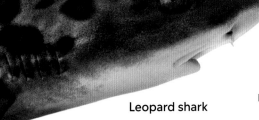

Port
Jackson
shark

DK LONDON

Senior Editor Carron Brown
Designer Chrissy Barnard
Senior US Editor Kayla Dugger
Managing Editor Francesca Baines
Managing Art Editor Philip Letsu
Production Editor Robert Dunn
Senior Production Controller Jude Crozier
Senior Jackets Designer Surabhi Wadhwa-Gandhi
Jacket Design Development Manager Sophia MTT
Publisher Andrew Macintyre
Associate Publishing Director Liz Wheeler
Art Director Karen Self
Publishing Director Jonathan Metcalf

Consultant Dr. James Thorburn

DK DELHI

Senior Editor Bharti Bedi
Senior Art Editor Vikas Chauhan
Art Editor Aparajita Sen
Picture Researcher Vishal Ghavri
Managing Editor Kingshuk Ghoshal
Managing Art Editor Govind Mittal
DTP Designers Pawan Kumar, Rakesh Kumar, Ashok Kumar
Jacket Designer Juhi Sheth

Fossil of
Ptychodus
tooth

Leopard shark

FIRST EDITION

Project Editor Marion Dent **Art Editor** Jill Plank
Senior Editor Helen Parker **Senior Art Editor** Julia Harris
Production Louise Barratt **Picture Research** Suzanne Williams
Special Photography Frank Greenaway, Dave King
Editorial Consultant Dr. Geoffrey Waller
Model Makers Graham High, Jeremy Hunt

Special Thanks Sea Life Centres (UK)

This Eyewitness ® Book has been conceived by
Dorling Kindersley Limited and Editions Gallimard

This American Edition, 2022
First American Edition, 1992
Published in the United States by DK Publishing
1745 Broadway, 20th Floor, New York, NY 10019

Dogfish
egg case

A catalog record for this book is available from the Library of Congress.

ISBN 978-0-7440-5640-2 (Paperback)
ISBN 978-0-7440-5641-9 (ALB)

DK books are available at special discounts when
purchased in bulk for sales promotions, premiums,
fund-raising, or educational use. For details, contact:
DK Publishing Special Markets,
1745 Broadway, 20th Floor, New York, NY 10019
SpecialSales@dk.com

Printed and bound in China

For the curious
www.dk.com

Shark rattle,
Samoa, South
Pacific

MIX
Paper from
responsible sources
FSC™ C018179

This book was made with Forest Stewardship Council™ certified
paper—one small step in DK's commitment to a sustainable future.
For more information go to www.dk.com/our-green-pledge

Contents

Model of a great white shark

What is a **shark?**

All sharks are cartilaginous fish, which means that they have skeletons made of gristlelike cartilage rather than bone. These skillful predators range from the dwarf lantern shark at about 8 in (20 cm) long to the whale shark, which can grow up to 40 ft (12 m).

Dorsal fin

Long, pointed snout

Mouth beneath snout, as in most sharks

Gill slits—most sharks have five

Pectoral fin—helps lift shark in water as it swims along and acts as a brake

Side view of a spinner shark—a classic shark shape

Saw sharks

Bramble sharks

Dogfish sharks

Rough sharks

Hammerhead sharks

Requiem sharks

Weasel sharks

Smooth-hounds

Barbeled hound shark

False cat shark

Finback cat sharks

Cat sharks

Long snout

Rounded body

Flattened body

Mouth below snout

Mouth at end of snout

Short snout

No anal fin

Angel sharks

Frilled shark

Cow sharks

Horn sharks

Anal fin

6–7 gill slits, 1 dorsal fin

5 gill slits, 2 dorsal fins

Fin spines

No fin spines

Mouth in front of eyes

Collared carpet sharks

Blind sharks

Wobbegongs

Bamboo sharks

Whale shark

Nurse shark

Zebra shark

Mouth behind eyes

Nictitating (blinking) eyelid; spiral valve in gut

No nictitating eyelid; ring valve in gut

Thresher sharks

Mackerel sharks

Basking sharks

Megamouth sharks

Crocodile sharks

Goblin sharks

Sand tigers

Classification of living sharks

There are more than 500 species of shark, which are placed in eight groups, or orders, based on body features. Classification may change when new sharks are discovered or when new relationships are revealed. For example, bramble sharks are often grouped with dogfish sharks, but they appear to be more closely related to angel sharks.

Thousands of teeth

During its lifetime, a shark will replace thousands of teeth. When the front ones wear out or break during feeding, they are replaced by larger, new ones growing in the row behind. Some sharks shed one or two teeth at a time, while others, like spiny dogfish and cookiecutters (p.45), replace a whole row at a time.

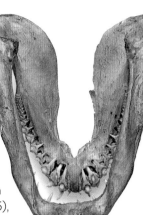

Jaws of sand tiger shark

Skin of bramble shark

Rough skin

Sharks are covered in toothlike scales called denticles, which give the skin a rough texture. Bramble sharks have large, thornlike denticles scattered over their skin (above) rather than covering the whole body.

Scales

Most bony fish have scales covering their skins. The scales increase in size as the fish grows.

Fish scale

Spinning around

When hunting in a school of fish, the spinner shark (left) spins in circles to confuse its prey. These sharks grow to 8 ft (2.5 m) long and live in the warm waters of the Atlantic, Indian, and Pacific Oceans.

Pelvic fin prevents shark from rolling

Small hook is similar to ones found on fossil sharks (p.13)

Anal fin

Tail, or caudal, fin

Ratfish

Chimaeras, or ratfish, are relatives of sharks and have ratlike tails and beaklike teeth.

Chimaera

(p.45)

FULL OF AIR

Bony fish have a swim, or air, bladder inside their bodies to prevent them from sinking. Sharks do not have swim bladders and most will sink if they stop swimming. Instead, they have oil-rich livers that reduce their weight in water and help control buoyancy.

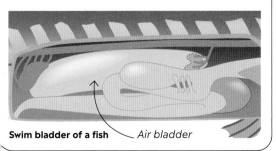

Swim bladder of a fish   *Air bladder*

Tail fin with same-size upper and lower lobes

Third dorsal fin

Second dorsal fin

First dorsal fin

Operculum, or covering for gills

Second anal fin

First anal fin

Pelvic fin

Barbel (feeler)

Pectoral fin

Side view of a bib

Shark or fish?

Shark skeletons (made of cartilage) are light and rubbery, while those of bony fish, such as the bib (above), are more rigid. Unlike sharks, bony fish have scales instead of denticles and a gill cover, or operculum, instead of gill slits. Bony fish also have a gas-filled swim bladder, which helps control buoyancy (keep the fish afloat).

Close relatives

A graceful manta ray swimming with slow beats of its huge wings looks nothing like a sleek reef shark. Yet rays and their cousins—skates, guitarfish, and sawfish—all belong to the same group as sharks. Most rays live on the sea bed where they feed on shellfish, worms, and fish.

The mighty manta
Manta rays measure up to 23 ft (7 m) across. This female manta, caught off the New Jersey coast, weighed more than 2,860 lb (1,300 kg).

Spines increase in size along body

Starry ray

Spotted ray

Blonde ray

Patterned bodies
Skates and rays have a great variety of patterns on their upper sides that help camouflage them on the sea bed. The undersides of rays' bodies are usually white.

Second dorsal fin

First dorsal fin

Painted ray

Guitarfish

Ray or skate?
Both rays and skates have flat bodies, but a ray's tail is more slender and whiplike. The major difference between the two is the way they reproduce (pp.20-23). While rays give birth to live young, skates lay eggs in the water.

Spines along back for extra protection against predators

Strange rays
Both guitarfish (50 species) and sawfish (five species) belong to the same group as rays. Guitarfish live mostly in warmer seas, while sawfish are also found in rivers and lakes. Sawfish use their "saws" for feeding and defense. They are one of the most threatened families of marine fishes in the world.

Sawfish

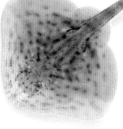

Baby skate
This baby skate can take more than eight years to mature and be able to reproduce.

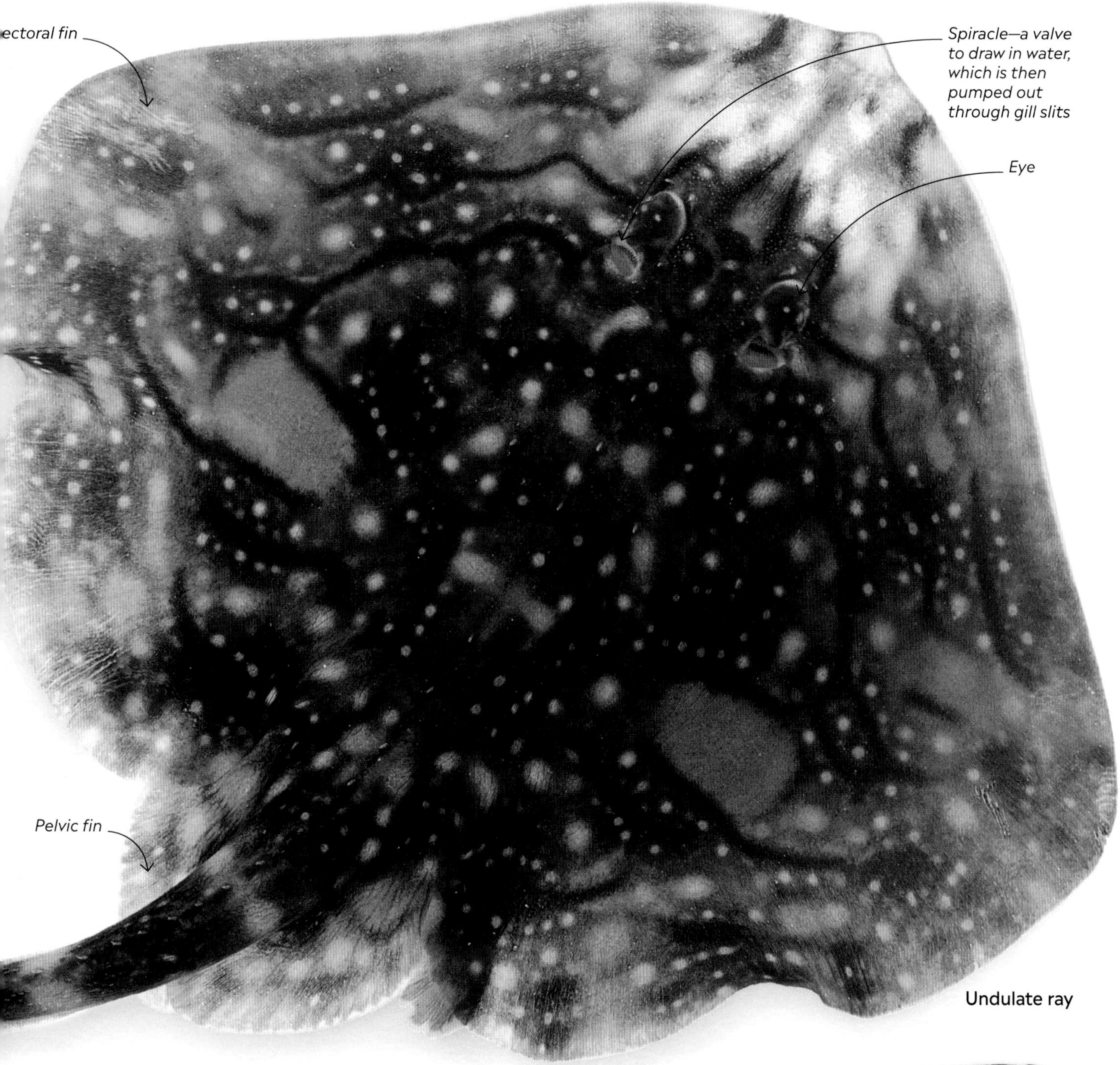

ectoral fin

Spiracle—a valve to draw in water, which is then pumped out through gill slits

Eye

Pelvic fin

Undulate ray

Sting

Stingray

There are more than 220 species of stingrays—found both in oceans and fresh water. Most are armed with one or more poisonous spines on their tails.

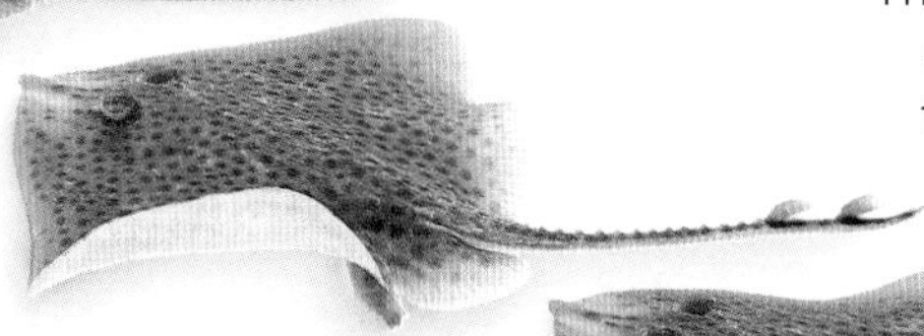

wimming

ost rays and skates swim using heir pectoral fins. But electric ays, sawfish, and some species of uitarfish swim as sharks do—by sculling with their ails. As rays swim along, they appear to fly through he water. The up-and-down motion of the pectoral ns is shown much better in species with huge ings, like the manta ray. These giant rays are ven able to leap out of the water.

Typical swimming sequence of rays

Inside a shark

Packaged inside this spinner shark's body are all the organs that keep it alive. Its gills help it breathe by taking in oxygen from the water and releasing carbon dioxide back into it. The heart pumps the blood around the body, while the stomach, liver, kidneys, and intestine all play a vital role in the digestive process. Large muscles in the body wall keep the shark swimming, while the skeleton and skin provide support. The brain controls the shark's actions, sending signals along the spinal cord. Finally, sharks, like all animals, cannot live forever and must reproduce to carry on the species. Female sharks produce eggs that develop into baby sharks, called pups. Some sharks lay their eggs in the water, while others give birth to live young (pp.20–23).

Scientists can tell the age of a shark by counting the rings in its backbone.

Paired kidneys regulate waste products

Ovary, where eggs are produced

Swimming muscles contract, sending a wave motion from head to tail

Model of a female spinner shark

Vent between claspers for disposing of body wastes

Clasper

Male shark

Rectal gland (third kidney) passes excess salt out of the body through the vent

Scroll valve in intestine— other sharks have spiral valves

Left lobe of liver

Caudal fin

Vertebral column

Cartilaginous rod

Claspers

All male sharks have a pair of claspers that are used in reproduction. Female sharks have an opening called a cloaca, through which body wastes are expelled.

Cloaca

Female shark (claspers absent)

All in the tail

Sharks have a backbone, or vertebral column, which extends into the upper lobe of their tail, or caudal fin. This type of caudal fin is called a heterocercal tail. The tail is strengthened by flexible rods of cartilage.

Sharks have a larger brain for their body size than most bony fish. The nasal sac, or sensory part of the nose, is close to the front part of the brain.

Nasal sac

Forebrain

Midbrain

Hindbrain

Brain of a lemon shark

Cartilage support of gill arch

Jaw-opening muscle pulls jaws forward

Nostril

Tongue is rigid, supported by a pad of cartilage

Jaw-closing muscle

Cartilage in floor of gullet

Gill arch

Heart

Blood

Blood collects in the first chamber of the shark's heart, then is pumped through the second and third, while the fourth prevents blood from flowing back into the heart. As water passes over the gills, oxygen is picked up and carbon dioxide released.

Pectoral girdle protects heart

Open gill slits

Shut gill slits

Open, shut

To breathe, water comes in through the shark's mouth, passes over the gills, and goes out of the gill slits. When the mouth opens, the gill slits shut. When it closes, the gill slits open.

Food processor

From the mouth, the food goes down the gullet into the stomach, where digestion begins, then into the intestine, where digested food is absorbed.

First dorsal fin

Stomach's descending limb

Pectoral fin

Second dorsal fin

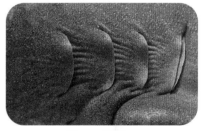

Rear view of whole body of shark

Anal fin

Wave motion in the muscles

Pelvic fin

Stomach's ascending limb

Spleen, producing red blood cells

Pancreas, producing chemicals called enzymes to digest food

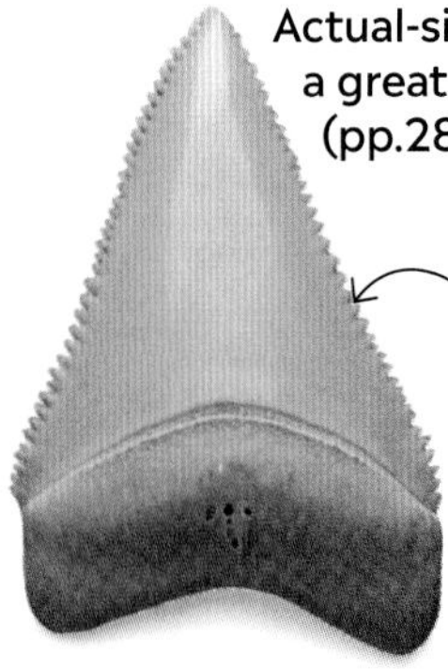

Actual-size tooth of
a great white shark
(pp.28-31)

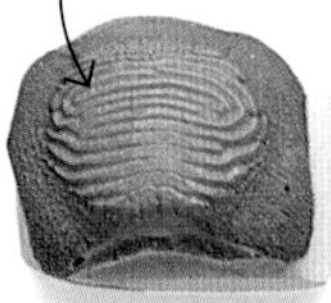

*Serrated edge
for cutting*

*Flat, ridged side
for crushing prey*

Tooth of
Ptychodus

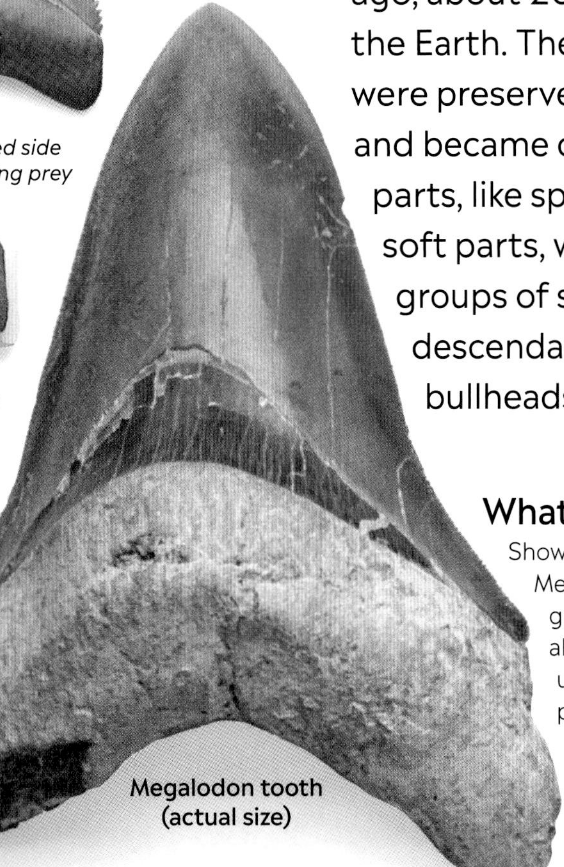

First sharks

The first sharks appeared in the seas 400 million years ago, about 200 million years before dinosaurs roamed the Earth. The remains of some of these early sharks were preserved as fossils when they fell to the sea bed and became covered with layers of sand and rock. Hard parts, like spines and teeth, fossilized more easily than soft parts, which often rotted away. The earliest groups of sharks became extinct, but the descendants of some groups, such as bullheads (pp.40–41), are alive today.

What big teeth!

Shown on the left is a fossil tooth of a Megalodon compared to one from a great white shark. Megalodon reached about 52 ft (16 m) long and probably used its teeth for slashing into large prey. The small, ridged tooth is from *Ptychodus*, which lived 120 million years ago.

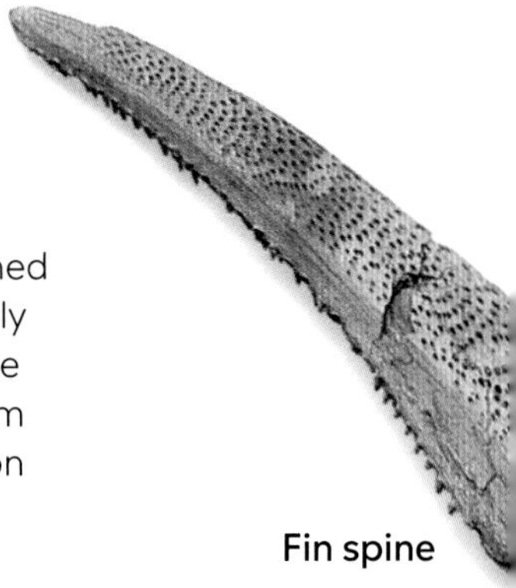

Megalodon tooth
(actual size)

Fin spine

Fossil from Lebanon

This lesser spotted dogfish died at least 65 million years ago. It is preserved in a piece of rock from the Lebanon in the Middle East.

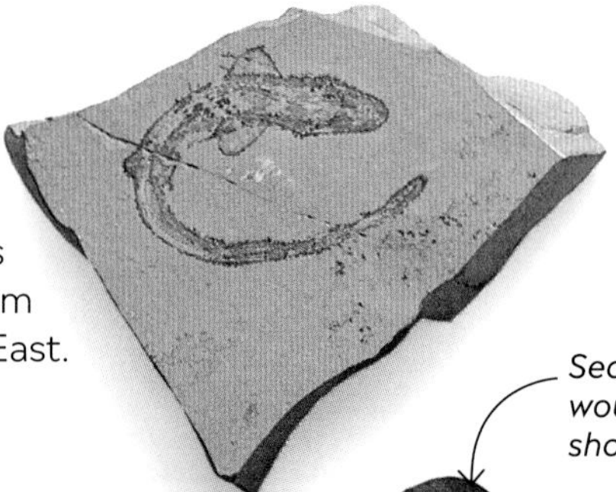

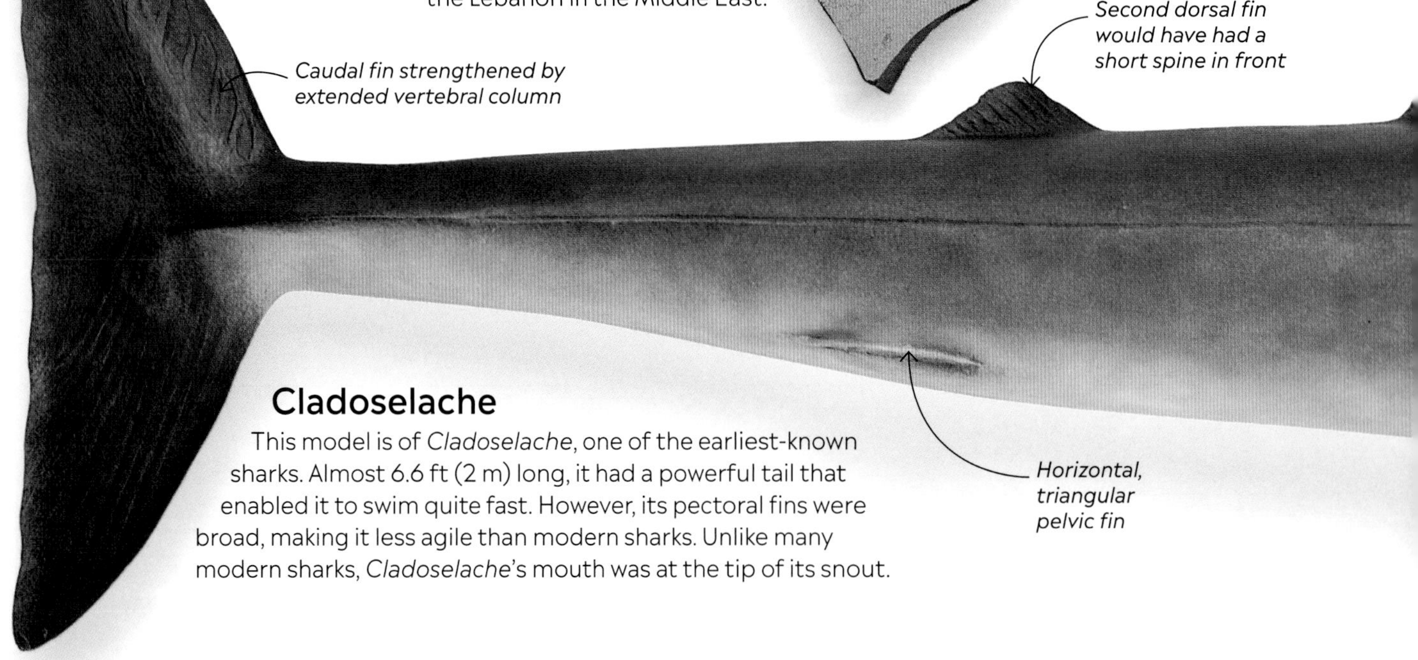

*Caudal fin strengthened by
extended vertebral column*

*Relatively small
dorsal fin also had
a spine in front*

*Second dorsal fin
would have had a
short spine in front*

Cladoselache

This model is of *Cladoselache*, one of the earliest-known sharks. Almost 6.6 ft (2 m) long, it had a powerful tail that enabled it to swim quite fast. However, its pectoral fins were broad, making it less agile than modern sharks. Unlike many modern sharks, *Cladoselache*'s mouth was at the tip of its snout.

*Horizontal,
triangular
pelvic fin*

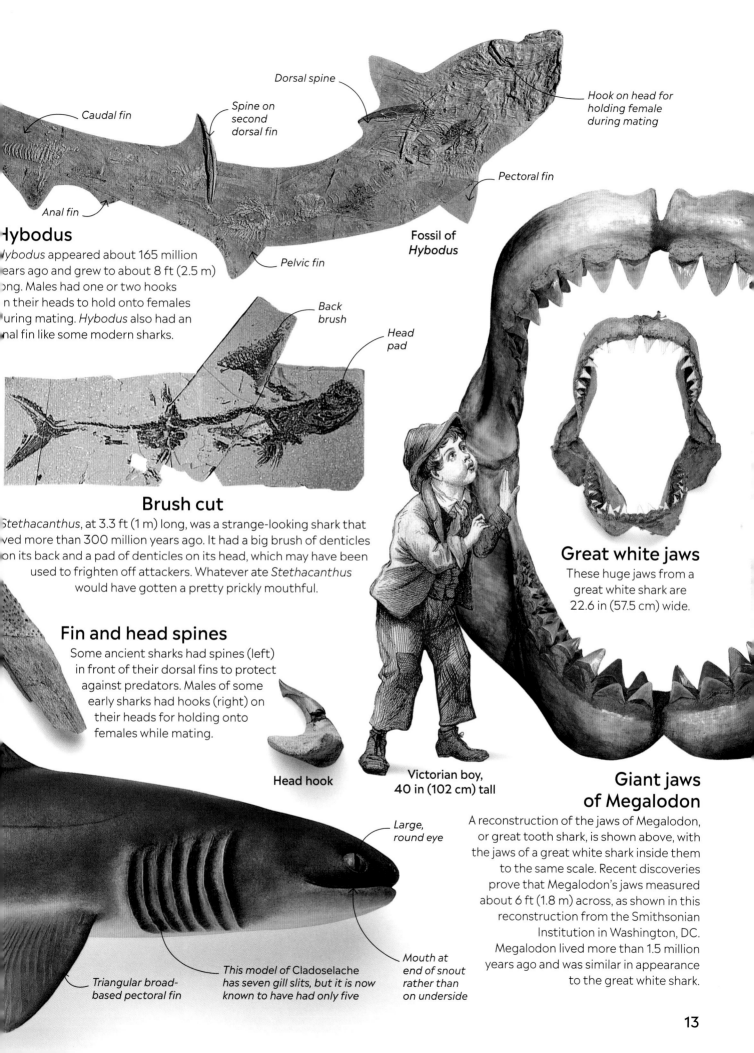

Caudal fin

Dorsal spine

Spine on second dorsal fin

Hook on head for holding female during mating

Pectoral fin

Anal fin

Hybodus

Hybodus appeared about 165 million years ago and grew to about 8 ft (2.5 m) long. Males had one or two hooks on their heads to hold onto females during mating. *Hybodus* also had an anal fin like some modern sharks.

Pelvic fin

Fossil of *Hybodus*

Back brush

Head pad

Brush cut

Stethacanthus, at 3.3 ft (1 m) long, was a strange-looking shark that lived more than 300 million years ago. It had a big brush of denticles on its back and a pad of denticles on its head, which may have been used to frighten off attackers. Whatever ate *Stethacanthus* would have gotten a pretty prickly mouthful.

Fin and head spines

Some ancient sharks had spines (left) in front of their dorsal fins to protect against predators. Males of some early sharks had hooks (right) on their heads for holding onto females while mating.

Head hook

Victorian boy, 40 in (102 cm) tall

Great white jaws

These huge jaws from a great white shark are 22.6 in (57.5 cm) wide.

Large, round eye

Mouth at end of snout rather than on underside

Triangular broad-based pectoral fin

This model of Cladoselache has seven gill slits, but it is now known to have had only five

Giant jaws of Megalodon

A reconstruction of the jaws of Megalodon, or great tooth shark, is shown above, with the jaws of a great white shark inside them to the same scale. Recent discoveries prove that Megalodon's jaws measured about 6 ft (1.8 m) across, as shown in this reconstruction from the Smithsonian Institution in Washington, DC. Megalodon lived more than 1.5 million years ago and was similar in appearance to the great white shark.

Amazing
grace

Sharks are graceful swimmers, propelling themselves through the water by beating their tails from side to side. Sharks use their pectoral fins to provide lift and change direction. By making changes to the angle of the fins, the shark can control whether it goes up, down, left, or right. Some sharks that live on the sea bed, such as horn sharks (pp.40–41) and epaulette sharks, can use their pectoral fins to crawl along the bottom. Unlike bony fish, sharks cannot move their pectoral fins like paddles, so they are unable to swim backward or hover in the water.

"S" shape
Sharks swim in a series of "S"-shaped curves.

Tail end
"S"-shaped waves pass down the shark's body, pushing it forward (above). The tail bends more than the rest of the body.

Denticles
The denticles on a shark's skin (p.7) line up with the direction of travel, helping reduce water resistance.

Cruising
The starry smooth-hound (right) uses its pectoral fins to stay level in the water. The two dorsal fins prevent the shark from rolling.

One-year-old leopard shark, 15 in (38 cm) long

See how it bends

Leopard sharks have flexible bodies, so they can turn around in small spaces. They spend much of their time cruising close to the sea bed.

Streamlined body

The large pectoral fins of the starry smooth-hound (left) are held straight out from the body to provide lift and keep the shark from sinking. When tilted, they can also act as brakes. The front edge of the fin is rounded and the rear edge is thin, so water flows over them more easily. The pointed snout and tapered body are streamlined to help the shark swim faster.

Full steam

A great white shark (above) normally swims at about 1.8 mph (3 kph). When closing in on a kill, the shark puts on a burst of speed of up to 15 mph (25 kph).

Turning point

Great whites are not nearly as flexible as smaller sharks. They have to surprise their prey to catch it.

15

Continued from previous page

Tails and more tails

The shape of a shark's tail depends on its lifestyle. Many sharks have tail fins where the upper lobe is larger than the lower. As the tail swings, this lobe produces lift that tends to push the shark's head down. To stop the shark from sinking, further lift is provided by the pectoral fins. In fast sharks, like the mako, the two lobes are almost equal in size. Slow bottom-dwellers, like the nurse shark, have less powerful tails and their swimming motion is more eel-like.

Upper lobe

Bonnethead's tail

The upper lobe of a bonnethead's tail is usually larger than the lower lobe. The lobe is held at an angle so that it is raised above the shark's midline (an imaginary line drawn from the tip of the shark's snout to the end of its body).

Lower lobe

Tail of a bonnethead shark

Thresher's tail

The upper lobe of a thresher's tail (left) is as long as its body. The tails of thresher sharks (p.59) are the longest of any shark and are used to stun prey.

Tail of a thresher shark

Keel helps the shark turn

Great white's tail

The upper and lower lobes of a great white's tail fin are almost equal in size. The keel on eith[er] side of the tail fin help[s] the big shark turn.

Tail view of a model of a great white shark (pp.28–31)

Angel shark

To lift its huge body off the sea bed, the angel shark beats its tail back and forth while tipping its large pectoral and pelvic fins for maximum lift.

Midair mako

Makos are probably the fastest sharks in the sea, reaching speeds of up to 28 mph (45 kph). When caught on an angler's line, they leap clear of the surface in an effort to escape (above). The mako's tail is the same shape as that of the tuna, another fast swimmer.

Lower lobe of angel shark's tail fin (pp.36-37) is longer than upper lobe

Angel sharks can **"crawl"** on the seafloor using their pectoral fins.

Nurse shark's tail

Slow-moving nurse sharks use their tails (right) for cruising along the sea bed.

Swell shark's tail

Swell sharks spend the day resting on the sea bed. Their tails (right) are held just above their midlines.

Horn shark's tail

The horn shark (right) is a slow swimmer. Its tail is held at a low angle to its midline.

Making sense

Sharks have the same five senses as people—sight, hearing, smell, taste, and touch. They also have a sixth electrical sense, which helps them locate prey and navigate. Under the water, light levels decrease with depth and sound travels five times faster. Sharks can detect vibrations made by animals moving through the water, giving them the sense called "distant touch."

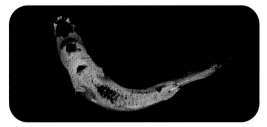

Glow in the dark

Many sharks, including the pygmy shark (above), are bioluminescent—special cells in their skin produce a soft blue light. These sharks regulate their light using hormones either to attract prey or to camouflage themselves from predators. In 2020, three species of deep-sea shark with bioluminescence were discovered by Belgian researcher Jérôme Mallefet.

Feeding frenzy

When sharks are feeding on bait, they often snap wildly at their food and bite each other.

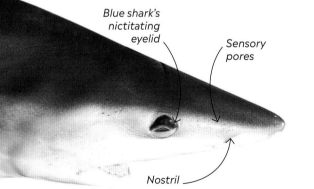

Blue shark's nictitating eyelid

Sensory pores

Nostril

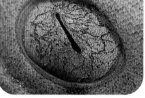

Epaulette's slit-shaped pupil

Dogfish with closed pupil

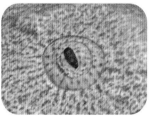

Angel shark's pupil

Reef shark with vertical pupil

Horn shark's pupil

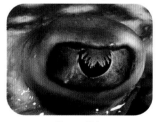

Ray with light-blocking screen

Eyes

In dim light, the pupils in a shark's eye expand to let in as much light as possible. In bright light, they narrow to tiny slits. The eye's retina, where images are focused, contains two types of cells—rods are sensitive to light changes, while cones help with detail and probably allow sharks to see in color. A special layer of cells called the tapetum lucidum helps sharks see in dim light.

Going to its head

The head contains the shark's major sense organs, including the sensory pores that are used to detect weak electrical signals. In some species, the eye is partly covered by a protective nictitating (blinking) eyelid or a nictitating membrane. As the shark swims, water flows through its nostrils, bringing a constant stream of odors.

Lateral line

Starry smooth-hound showing lateral line

Distant touch

Sharks have a line of special cells along the length of their body, called the lateral line. These cells detect vibrations in the water.

Eyes on stalks

Hammerheads' eyes are set on either side of their head projections, giving them a wide field of vision. The nostrils are widely spaced on the front of the head, helping them detect where a smell is coming from.

Compass

Imaginary magnet

North–south axis

Earth's magnetic field

Compass sense

Some sharks migrate hundreds of miles (km). Scientists think sharks have a "compass sense" to guide them and also use their sense of smell to navigate. They may be able to navigate by sensing changes in their own electric fields in relation to the Earth's magnetic field. Corrections have to be made for speed and direction of ocean currents, which could sweep the shark off course.

Duck-billed platypus

Like the shark, the Australian duck-billed platypus can also detect electrical signals from its prey, using receptors on the left-hand side of its bill. Platypuses live in streams, where they hunt for insects and other small creatures.

THE INNER EAR

Sharks' ears are inside their heads on either side of the brain case. The three semicircular canals placed at right angles to each other help the shark work out which way it has turned in the water. Receptors in the inner ear pick up sounds traveling through the water.

Semicircular canal, one of three

Nurse shark

Barbel

Barbels

The pair of feelers, or barbels, on the nurse shark's nose (right) means it can feel vibrations from prey hiding in the sand. Barbels may also help sharks smell and taste prey.

Spotted nose

The spots on this sand tiger's snout are sensory pores called ampullae of Lorenzini. Full of jelly, the pores detect weak electrical signals, helping the shark find prey at close range. The presence of metal in the ocean can confuse this sense, sometimes causing sharks to bite boats.

Nostril

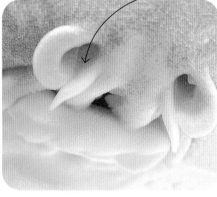

Nice nose

Water is taken in through the epaulette's big nostrils and passed to a nasal sac where smells are detected.

Snout of an epaulette shark

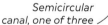

Reproduction

Sharks produce young in three ways. Some female sharks are viviparous, which means that they give birth to baby sharks called pups (pp.22–23). Other sharks are oviparous, which means that they lay eggs in the water. The eggs are encased in a leathery shell and deposited on the sea bed. Once the eggs are laid, the female swims away, leaving them to develop and hatch on their own. Most sharks, however, are ovoviviparous, which means that the young develop inside eggs but hatch while they are still inside the mother.

Spiral egg case
The horn shark wedges its egg case into rocks to protect it.

Holding on
The egg case of the dogfish, or cat shark, is firmly anchored onto anything growing on the sea bed to keep it from being swept away.

Catch me if you can
This male white tip reef shark is chasing a female in the hope that she will mate with him. He may be attracted by her smell.

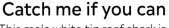

Keeping close
The male white tip reef shark bites the female to encourage her to mate. He holds her pectoral fin in his jaws to keep her close during mating.

Thick skins
Female blue sharks have much thicker skins than males, preventing serious injury during courtship.

Mating
People rarely see sharks mating in the wild, or even in aquariums. It seems that larger sharks mate side to side, while smaller male sharks wrap themselves around the female when mating.

Tendril

Dogfish eggs

Baby dogfish, or embryos, lie safe inside their egg cases, which are anchored onto seaweed by tendrils. The embryos take about nine months to develop before they hatch. During this time, each embryo gets its nourishment from its large yolk sac.

Dogfish embryo

Pair of 10-day-old dogfish

Yolk sac

Pair of dogfish egg cases

Cream-colored underside

Young dogfish

These young dogfish are 10 days old. Although they are only 4 in (10 cm) long, they look like small versions of their parents. Shark pups are generally much larger and more developed than the young of bony fish.

One-month-old swell shark embryo

The female swell shark lays two eggs at a [ti]me in clumps of seaweed. Each egg is protected [in] a leathery case. After a month, the egg has [de]veloped a tiny embryo, which draws its [no]urishment from its large yolk sac.

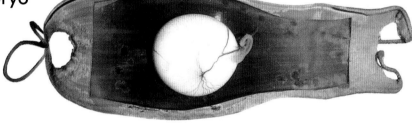

Coloring consists of [li]ght and dark brown [ba]nds, with dark spots on shark's top side

2 Three-month-old embryo

The embryo now has eyes and a tail. Oxygen in the water passes through the egg case so that the embryo can breathe.

3 Seven-month-old embryo

By now, the embryo has a complete set of fins. The baby shark, or pup, will hatch as soon as it has used up the rest of the yolk sac.

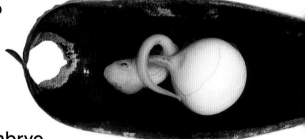

4 Two-month-old pup

After 10 months, the young swell shark—at 6 in (15 cm) long—has hatched from the egg case. Its mottled color pattern makes it hard for predators to see where it is hiding on the sea bed.

Two-month-old swell shark pup

Live **young**

The majority of sharks give birth to live young instead of laying eggs (pp.20–21). Most female sharks are ovoviviparous, producing large, yolky eggs that develop inside their body. The developing pup, or embryo, is fed by a yolk sac attached to its belly. When this is used up, the pup is ready to be born. In viviparous sharks, such as lemon, blue, bull, and hammerhead sharks, nourishment from the mother's blood passes to the embryo through a tube called the umbilical cord.

Mother and baby
Humans look after their babies, but shark pups must fend for themselves as soon as they are born.

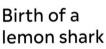

Birth of a lemon shark
(1) Lemon sharks come into shallow coastal lagoons, which are sheltered from the waves, to give birth. The tip of the pup's tail is just visible poking out of its mother.
(2) Here, the female has begun to give birth.
(3) The scientist is helping the pup pass out of the mother's birth canal.

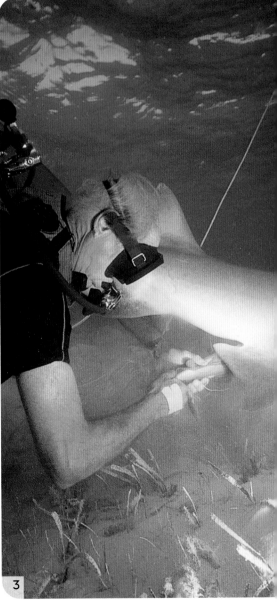

Baby African elephant

A baby elephant takes 22 months to gestate (develop inside its mother's body). The spiny dogfish has a similar gestation period of between 18 and 24 months.

Hammerheads

Hammerhead sharks can give birth to up to 40 pups at a time. While in the womb, each pup is connected to its mother by an umbilical cord.

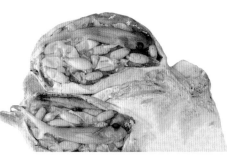

Bigeye thresher pup

As a bigeye thresher pup develops inside the womb, it feeds on eggs produced by its mother.

Spiny babies

Just as spines on hedgehog babies emerge after birth, those on baby spiny dogfish have special coverings that protect their mother.

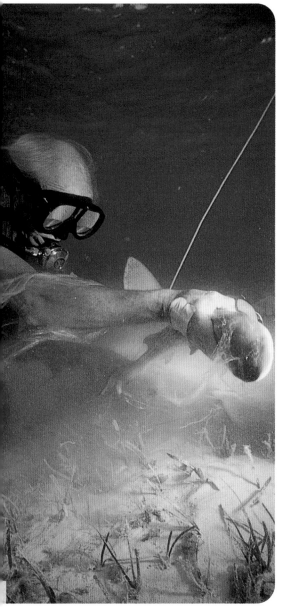

(4) The lemon shark pup is still attached to its mother by the umbilical cord.
(5) The pup rests before swimming away and breaking the umbilical cord.
(6) It faces life on its own, hiding from predators in mangrove roots. For many years, it will stay in a small nursery area in the lagoon, near where it was born. Then it will make trips out of the lagoon to the coral reefs and farther afield.

5

6

Teeth and **diet**

Sharks constantly lose their teeth. When the front ones wear out, they are replaced by new ones growing in another row behind. Sharks' teeth come in many shapes and sizes and have different uses. Spiked teeth are used for gripping small prey, while serrated (sawlike) teeth are used for cutting. Long, curved teeth get a hold of slippery fish, while blunt teeth crunch up shellfish. A few species of shark, like basking sharks (pp.34–35), filter their food from the water.

Epaulette eating

Epaulette sharks use their pectoral fins to crawl among coral reefs. They feed on small fish, crabs, and shrimp found in shallows and tidepools.

Epaulette shark

Mouth of swell shark

Crunchy diet

Port Jackson sharks have strong back teeth to crush hard-shelled crabs, mussels, and sea urchins.

Mussels

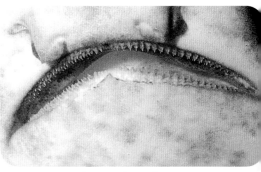

Mouth of Port Jackson

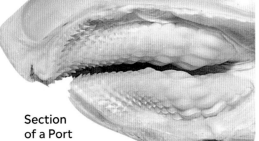

Section of a Port Jackson's jaws

Sea urchin

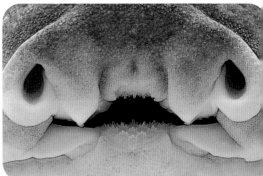

Smile, please

Swell sharks (top) have big mouths armed with rows of tiny teeth. The Port Jackson shark (above) has rows of small front teeth that are visible when its mouth is open.

Daily menu

Tiger sharks cruise warm waters. Their varied diet includes jellyfish, shelled turtles, and poisonous sea snakes. Sea birds are not safe, as tiger sharks will grab them from the surface of the sea. Occasionally, they attack humans.

All the better to eat with

Tiger sharks have multipurpose teeth. The pointed tip grips prey, while the serrated bottom edges are for cutting.

Jaws

A tiger shark's jaws are only loosely connected to its skull, allowing the shark to push out its jaws and take a big bite.

Sea turtle

Tiger mouth

Tiger sharks often move inshore at night to feed.

Dish of the day

Sand tigers eat a variety of bony fish (left), rays, and lobsters.

Goatfish

Lobster

Ragged tooth shark

Sand tigers, called ragged tooth sharks in South Africa and gray nurse sharks in Australia, grow to 10 ft (3 m). Their long, curved teeth get smaller toward the sides of the jaw and are ideal for snaring fish or squid.

Claws

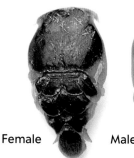

Claw

Antenna

Head

Body section

Abdomen

This copepod (¾ in/ 1.9 cm long) digs its sharp claws into a basking shark's skin. It feeds on the shark's skin and blood.

Friend or **foe?**

Like most animals, sharks have a variety of small friends and enemies that choose to live on or within them. Remora fish often hitch a ride using suckers on their heads to attach themselves to the shark. Other kinds of fish, called pilot fish, swim alongside sharks. Parasites, such as copepods and barnacles, feed on sharks' skin and blood. They may cause discomfort, but they rarely kill the shark.

Barnacles

Soft shell

Root, or stalk

Rootlet for absorbing nutrients

The larvae, or young, of the barnacle attach themselves to the dorsal fins of spurdogs or dogfish. Rootlets on the stalk absorb nutrients from the shark.

Clean teeth

Other animals have friends, too. This bird is cleaning a crocodile's teeth.

Female   **Male**

Cling-ons

These copepods (½ in/1.3 cm long) have sticky pads to fasten onto sharks' fins.

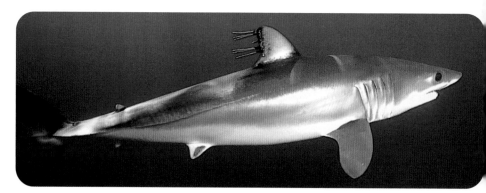

Streamers

Copepods cling onto the dorsal fins of this mako shark (above). The egg cases streaming out behind them contain a stack of disk-shaped eggs. When the eggs are released, they hatch into tiny young, or larvae.

Remoras

Found in tropical oceans, the remora (left) has a ridged sucker on the top of its head to attach itself to sharks and rays. While hitching a ride, remoras may do their hosts a favor by nibbling off skin parasites.

Pilot fish

Young golden trevally from the Pacific Ocean swim with larger fish, including sharks. This helps them gain protection from predators, as other fish tend to avoid sharks. Despite their name, pilot fish do not guide sharks to food.

Anchor that embeds in eye's surface

Arm

Head

Trunk

Eye spy

This strange copepod (left) hangs by its arms to a Greenland shark's eye. It feeds on the eye's surface, but once there, it cannot let go.

Egg sac, containing thousands of eggs

Mobile home

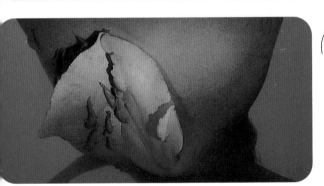

Whale sharks (top) are so big that they provide living space for large numbers of remoras. Some remoras gather around the shark's mouth and gills, where they feed on parasites; others nestle near the cloaca (p.10) on a female shark (above).

Tentacle

Head

Body

Tapeworms

Hundreds of 1-ft (30-cm) tapeworms may live in a shark's gut, where they absorb food through their body. The worms anchor themselves to the gut using spiny tentacles.

Navigating

This ship is guided into harbor by pilot boats, but sharks navigate on their own (pp.18–19).

Great white shark

A powerful predator, this awesome shark grows to at least 20 ft (6 m) long and weighs more than 2.2 tons (2 metric tons). It is the largest of the predatory sharks, capable of eating sea lions whole. Great whites occasionally attack humans (pp.48–49), usually having mistaken them for seals. It is thought that great whites may interact with one another, slapping their tails against the water to ward each other off.

Dorsal fin

Small second dorsal fin, compared to size of first dorsal fin

Pelvic fin

Long snout

Front view of model of a great white shark

Swimming keel

Warm blood
Great whites and their relatives—the mako, thresher, and porbeagle—are all warm-blooded, which means that they are able to keep their body temperature higher than the surrounding water. A high body temperature means that great whites have warm muscles that are able to act quickly. This is important for a predator that has to make a high-speed dash to catch its prey.

Upper and lower lobes of tail fin are almost symmetrical (pp.16–17)

Relatively small anal fin

Clasper

Taking the bait
Scientists, filmmakers, and photographers use a mixture of oil, blood, tuna, and mackerel to attract great whites. As the shark takes the bait, its eyes roll back in their sockets, revealing the white surface of the eyeball. This protects the more vital front part of the eye from being scratched by its prey.

White death

[A] great white's coloring makes it difficult to see [in] the water, so it is able to sneak up on its victims. [W]hen seen from below, this shark's white undersides [lo]ok like a patch of sunlight at the water's surface. [T]his is called countershading camouflage. The shark [is] sometimes called a "white pointer," referring [to] its pointed snout, which makes it [m]ore streamlined.

Long gill slit— one of five

Pore marking position of ampullae of Lorenzini (p.19)

Sharp, serrated teeth

Full length side view of model of a male great white shark

Pectoral fin

Tagging a great white

A scientist tags a great white (pp.56-57). Satellite tags show that great whites can cruise at 1.8 mph (3 kph), traveling about 124 miles (200 km) in three days.

Continued from previous page

0 miles
(0 km)

1,250 miles
(2,000 km)

2,500 miles
(4,000 km)

3,730 miles
(6,000 km)

Distribution of great white sharks

White Shark Café

For more than 25 years, Dr. Barbara Block (pictured here with the tags she places on the sharks) and her team have been tagging great white sharks to track their migration. Her study has revealed that each year great white sharks congregate in large numbers in an area off California called the White Shark Café. Although it is not known for sure why they gather in the area, it may be linked to an abundance of prey.

What a great white eats

Great white sharks live in cool to warm waters throughout the world. They often hunt near seal colonies, where they prey on both adults and young. When hunting a seal, a great white charges through the water, then attacks from below—sometimes even leaping into the air. The shark may release its victim before returning to finish it off. The great white's diet changes as it grows up. Young sharks eat mostly fish, while older sharks tackle larger prey such as sea lions.

Young elephar
seals are easy pre

On the menu

Great whites eat a variety of animals, including bony fish; other sharks; some sea birds; marine mammals, such as seals and porpoises; and, occasionally, people! They also eat whale carcasses and other dead animals.

Great whites are known to attack South African penguins

Young great whites prey on North American leopard sharks (above)

Young great whites eat bony fish, such as cabezon (left)

Californian sea lions are eaten by adult great whites

Big bite

This great white's upper jaw juts forward and its snout is tipped upward so it can grab a big chunk of meat.

A great white shark can leap about 10 ft (3 m) out of the water.

Distribution of whale sharks

3,730 miles (6,000 km)
2,500 miles (4,000 km)
1,250 miles (2,000 km)
0 miles (0 km)

Not much of a bite

Whale sharks do not bite or chew, so they do not need their tiny teeth.

At the dentis[t]

Humans need t[o] replace lost teet[h] with false ones i[n] order to chew food. All shark[s], even those tha[t] don't bite or che[w], continuously gro[w] new teet[h].

Gentle giants

Whale sharks are the largest fish in the world, reaching lengths of at least 40 ft (12 m) and weighing 14.6 tons (13.2 metric tons). These harmless giants can cruise at 1.9 mph (3 kph), often near the surface of the water, and dive down to depths of up to 5,900 ft (1,800 m). They live in warm, tropical waters in places where there is a good supply of food to support their large bulk. They feed by filtering food out of the water. Whale sharks give birth to as many as 300 pups, hatched from eggs inside their bodies (pp.20–23).

Each whale shark has a unique set of spots that can be used to identify it.

A great gulp

Despite their great size, whale sharks feed on plankton (small plants and animals that drift in the sea), small fish, and squid. As the sea water passes through their huge mouths, food is strained through bristly filters called gill rakers. Other large fish, such as basking sharks (pp.34–35), manta rays (pp.8-9), megamouths (pp.44–45), and baleen whales, also feed by filtering food out of the water.

Epaulette sharks grow to 3.3 ft (1 m) long

Brown-banded bamboo sharks grow to just over 3.3 ft (1 m) long

Anal fin

White-spotted bamboo sharks grow to about 37 in (95 cm) long

Humpback whales

Whale sharks are named after those other ocean giants—the whales.

One big happy family

Although they are much smaller, these four sharks (white-spotted and brown-banded bamboos, epaulette, and nurse) all belong to the same group as the whale shark. They all have two barbels on their snouts that help them find food buried in the sea bed.

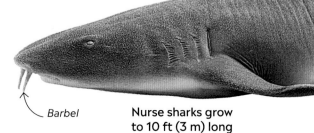

Barbel

Nurse sharks grow to 10 ft (3 m) long

Basking
beauties

Cruising along with their huge mouths wide open to filter food, basking sharks are like giant mobile sieves. The second largest fish in the world, after the whale shark (pp.32–33), basking sharks grow to about 33 ft (10 m) long and weigh over 4.4 tons (4 metric tons). They often swim at the surface on sunny days with their dorsal fins out of the water. They used to make easy targets for fishermen who caught them for their large fins, meat, and the oil in their livers—which may be a quarter of the shark's body weight.

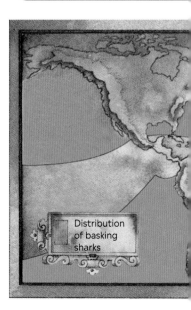

Oily mouths
Oil from sharks' livers has been used in cosmetics such as lipstick.

Open mouth of basking shark

Shark fishing
This basking shark was caught at Achill Island off the coast of Ireland. Fishing stopped when the numbers of sharks declined.

👁 EYEWITNESS

Demystifying behavior
In 1995, British marine ecologist David Sims tracked a group of around 20 basking sharks by attaching satellite tags to them. He found that the sharks travel great distances during some months of the year to feed on a specific type of plankton. This study disproved the 50-year-old assumption that basking sharks hibernate during winter.

Distribution of basking sharks

Open mouthed

As the basking shark swims, 330,000 gallons (1.5 million liters) of water flow through its huge mouth each hour. Drifting in the water are tiny creatures known as plankton (above), which are strained out of the water by hundreds of bristly gill rakers (p.24) and trapped in a layer of slime. After a minute, the shark closes its mouth, emptying the water out through its gill slits before swallowing its food. Basking sharks may migrate several thousand miles (km) in search of good supplies of plankton.

0 miles (0 km)

1,250 miles (2,000 km)

2,500 miles (4,000 km)

3,730 miles (6,000 km)

Angel sharks

The 16 species of angel shark have flattened bodies and broad pectoral fins that look like angels' wings. These strange sharks hide on the sea bed waiting to ambush prey with their snapping jaws. Found in shallow coastal waters, angel sharks swim like other sharks, using their large tails to propel themselves forward.

Monk fish

Angel sharks are also known as "monk fish" because the shape of their heads looks like the hood on a monk's cloak.

Lower lobe of tail is longer than the upper lobe—a feature unique to angel sharks

Second dorsal fin

| 0 miles (0 km) | 1,250 miles (2,000 km) | 2,500 miles (4,000 km) | 3,730 miles (6,000 km) |

Distribution of angel sharks

Pelvic fin

First dorsal fin

Gill slit

Mouth

Eye

Spiracle

Pelvic fin

Underside of ray

Lookalikes

Rays are flat like angel sharks, but their pectoral fins are joined to their head and their gill slits are on the underside of the body.

Pectoral fin

Top side of ray

Angels

This angel shark grows up to 6.5 ft (2 m) long. It is found in the Mediterranean and Baltic Seas, the eastern Atlantic Ocean, and the English Channel. To get oxygen, the angel shark draws in water through the large spiracles on the top of its head. Water drawn through the spiracles is more likely to be free of silt than water taken in through the mouth.

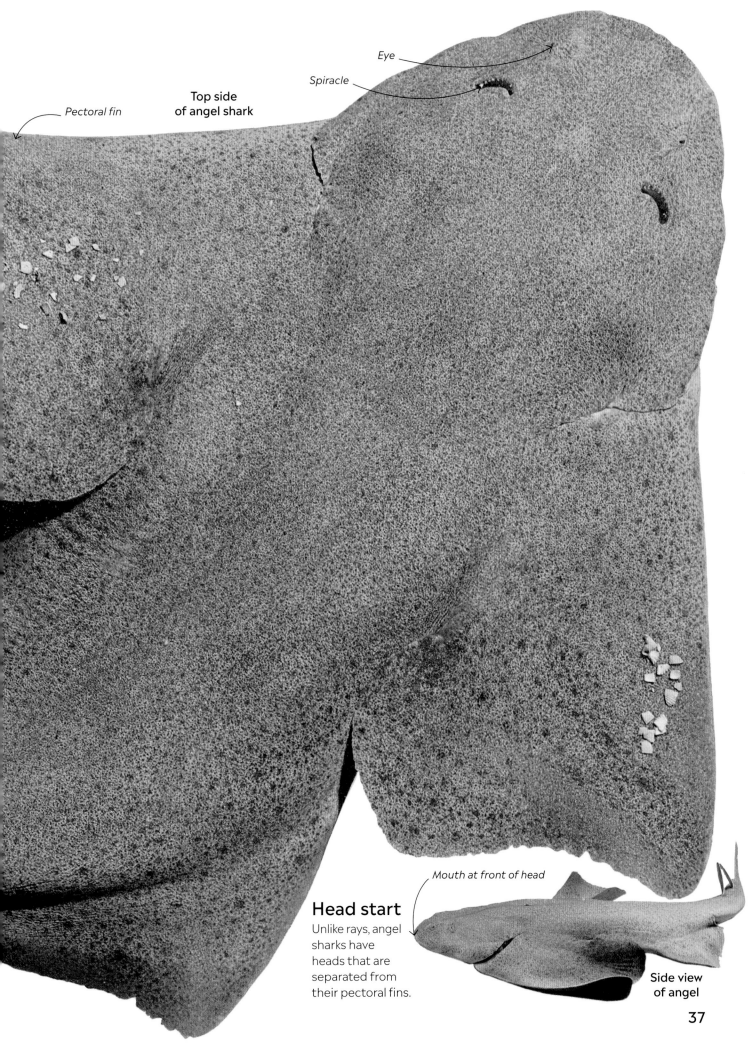

Pectoral fin

Top side of angel shark

Eye

Spiracle

Mouth at front of head

Head start

Unlike rays, angel sharks have heads that are separated from their pectoral fins.

Side view of angel

37

Japanese
wobbegong

Continued from previous page

Secret agent
Like undercover spies,
some sharks disguise
themselves to hide
from predators.

— Lobe

— Barbel

Japanese wobbegong
This shark grows to about 3.3 ft
(1 m). Wobbegongs are not
usually aggressive, but people
have been bitten when they have
stepped on one by mistake.

Undercover sharks
Many bottom-dwelling sharks use
camouflage to help them blend
in with their surroundings. They
have blotches, spots, or stripes
that make them difficult to see
on the sea bed. Wobbegongs
have blotchy skins and lobes on
their heads that look like bits
of seaweed. Swell sharks
hide in crevices, while
angel sharks cover
themselves with sand.
These undercover sharks
often lie in wait for prey to move
close, then snap them up. Smaller
sharks use camouflage to avoid
being eaten by larger predators.

Sand disguise
It is difficult to
see angel
sharks (pp.36-
37) lying on the sea bed
because they are flattened
and their mottled skin
looks like sand (top left). To
complete their disguise,
they shuffle their pectoral
fins to bury their bodies in
sand (center left). Their
eyes poke above the
surface of the sand
(bottom left)
watching for prey.
When a fish
comes close,
the angel shark
lunges forward, snapping
its jaws shut around it.

Bearded disguise
The branched lobes around the
tasselled wobbegong's mouth
look like seaweed to
unsuspecting prey.

Mug shots

This ornate wobbegong looks different from various angles—from above (top left) and from the side (bottom left). The wobbegong's disguise works just as well from any direction.

Predators may not see a swell shark because it is well camouflaged.

Ornate wobbegong

Barbel

Night feeder

The tasselled wobbegong feeds mainly at night. It lurks among the coral and seaweed, waiting to ambush its prey.

life on the sea bed

Wobbegongs spend much of the day lurking on the sea bed. Like angel sharks, they have flattened bodies with eyes and spiracles on the top of their heads. The seaweedlike barbels on the snout are used to attract prey.

Lobe

Horn sharks

Horn sharks get their name from the two horn-shaped spines on their backs. They are also known as bullheads because they have broad heads with ridges above the eyes. The nine species of horn shark are found in the Pacific and Indian Oceans, where they live on the sea bed in shallow water. They swim with slow beats of their tails and push themselves along the bottom with their pectoral fins. Sadly, horn sharks are often killed for their spines, which are used to make jewelry.

Pelvic fin

A pair of swimming Port Jackson sharks, which are named after a harbor in Australia

Heap of horns

Port Jackson sharks often rest in groups during the day. Favorite rest sites are the sandy floors of caves or the channels between rocks. At night, they search for food such as sea urchins and starfish.

Spine in front of first dorsal fin

Spine of second dorsal fin

Caudal (tail) fin

Typical spotted pattern on skin

Eye

Side view of horn shark

Pelvic fin

Gill slit

Eye

Pig headed

Port Jackson sharks are often called "pig fish" because of their blunt heads and big nostrils. They are also called bulldog sharks because their squashed-up snouts make them look like bulldogs. These sharks like to feed on oysters, which they crunch with their strong back teeth.

Nostril

Pectoral fin

Spine on first dorsal fin

Spine on second dorsal fin—Port Jackson sharks are often killed for their spines

Anal fin

Caudal fin

Broad, dark stripe on skin, typical of Port Jackson shark

Pelvic fin

Nostril

Front view of Port Jackson shark

Horn sharks

Some horn sharks feed on purple sea urchins. The purple pigment, or color, is not broken down when the shark digests its food. Instead, the pigment stains the shark's teeth and spines purple.

Developed nostrils

Horn sharks, like this Port Jackson, have good sense of smell, which may help them find food. They have blunt teeth at the back of their jaws for crushing the shells of their prey.

Hammerheads

Of all the sharks, hammerheads have the strangest-shaped heads. The 10 species of hammerhead include the bonnetheads and the wingheads, whose heads can grow as wide as half the length of their bodies. Scalloped hammerheads are found in warm waters throughout the world. They gather in large groups, called schools, around seamounts (underwater mountains or volcanoes).

Blue-spotted stingray

Dorsal fin

Gill slit

Mouth

Anal fin

Pelvic fin

Pectoral fin

A fine bonnet

Bonnetheads are the smallest of the hammerheads, reaching only 5 ft (1.5 m) long.

Difficult diet

Stingrays are the favorite food of the great hammerhead, even though their tails are armed with venomous spines, or "stings."

Head on

Hammerheads' eyes are at the tips of their "hammers," giving them an excellent view as they swing their heads from side to side. They also use their ampullae of Lorenzini (p.19) to help them locate prey.

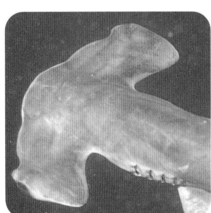

Two different sharks

The shape of the hammerhead's head (top) compared to that of other sharks, like the tope (bottom), fascinated early naturalists.

Dorsal fin

Eye

Hammerhead schools

Hammerheads often swim in schools of hundreds of sharks, but the reason why they group together is unclear. These large predators have few enemies, so it is unlikely they gather for protection.

Why a hammer?

No one knows why a hammerhead has a
hammer-shaped head, but the broad, flattened
head may give extra lift to the front of the
shark's body as it swims.

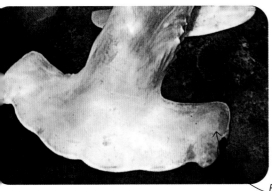

— Flat, wide head

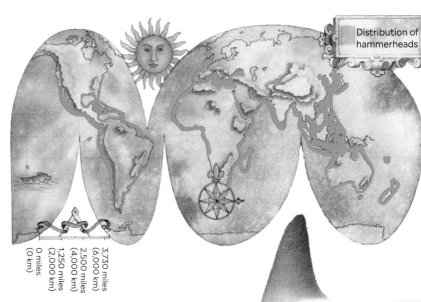

0 miles
(0 km)

1,250 miles
(2,000 km)

2,500 miles
(4,000 km)

3,730 miles
(6,000 km)

The bonnethead shark is the
irst known omnivorous
species of shark.

Scalloped
hammerhead

Weird and wonderful

The megamouth, one of the world's most extraordinary sharks, was discovered only in 1976. No one had seen this large shark before, although it is more than 16 ft (5 m) long and weighs 1,500 lb (680 kg). Since 1976, more than 55 megamouths have been found, including one that was captured alive off the coast of California in 1990. Another strange shark, the goblin shark, lives in deep water and is rarely seen alive. Other mysteries have been solved. No one knew what caused circular bites on whales, dolphins, and seals, but the culprits were found to be cookiecutter sharks.

Big mouth

Megamouth is named after its huge mouth, which can measure up to 3 ft (1 m) wide. It feeds on animal plankton, attracting prey with luminous (glowing) organs around its lips. The fir megamouth was four entangled in the anchor of a US naval boat off Hawaii.

REALLY WEIRD

Goblin sharks were discovered off the coast of Japan in 1898. They grow to 10 ft (3 m) long and live in deep water down to at least 4,265 ft (1,300 m).

Long snout with sensory pores for detecting prey

Goblin shark

Top side of goblin shark's head

Underside of goblin shark's head

EYEWITNESS

Longest-living vertebrate
In 2016, Dr. Julius Nielson (below) led a team at the University of Copenhagen, Denmark, that determined that Greenland sharks can live for several hundred years. The eye lens of a Greenland shark is layered like an onion. The team studied the layers that formed when the shark was a pup to determine its age.

Glows in the dark
The lantern shark lives in the oceans' depths. They are called lantern sharks because they glow in the dark. Among the world's smallest sharks, they grow to only 8 in (20 cm) long.

Distribution of cookiecutters

Bite-size

Cookiecutters, only 1.6 ft (0.5 m) long, have large teeth for sharks. They use their sawlike teeth to cut out oval-shaped chunks of flesh from whales, seals, dolphins, and other large fish.

Goddess of light

The cookiecutters' scientific name is *Isistius brasiliensis* after Isis, the Egyptian goddess of light. The sharks have glowing light organs on their bellies, which may attract prey, such as whales, to come close enough to be bitten.

Bitten

Cookiecutter sharks made the wounds on this seal.

Shark artifacts

Early people made tools from sharks' teeth, while the skin was used to make shoes and grips for weapons (p.60). Fishing for sharks with primitive tools was difficult and dangerous, and stories and legends about sharks were common among seafaring people. Today, there are many modern alternatives to using shark teeth and skin, helping reduce the demand for shark products.

Large, serrated tooth, probably from a great white shark (pp.28-31)

Tooth necklace
The 10 teeth in this decorativ necklace probably came fron great white sharks caught b Maoris off the coast of New Zealand.

Monkey
The teeth of this Mexican monkey head are taken from a shark.

Shark-shaped gold weight from Ghana, West Africa

Shoes made of shark skin from India

Tin toy from Malaysia

Shark tooth

Shark tooth

Tool, tipped with a shark's tooth

Shark skin

Wooden scraper, covered in shark skin, from Santa Cruz in the Pacific

Shark skin

18th-centu wooden drum, mad with shark skin, from the Hawaiia Islands

Shark skin grater (below) from the Wallis Islands in the Pacific

Wooden knife (right) made with sharks' teeth from Greenland

Shark skin

Sharks in the home
From ancient times, the skins and teeth of sharks have been used to make a variety of household items, such as food graters, knives, and tools. The soft skin can be used like leather for making shoes, belts, or even drums (above).

Fishing and worship

In some South Pacific islands, boys would catch sharks using rattles (right), nooses, harpoons, and hooks. The Hawaiian islanders believed that their dead relatives came back to life in the form of animals, such as sharks. These shark spirits would protect them while fishing. On other Pacific islands, sharks were thought of as gods.

Long spear for catching sharks from the Nicobar Islands, India

Coconut rattle for attracting sharks

Small harpoon for catching sharks

Shark-tooth necklace from New Zealand

Hooks for catching sharks

Wood

Shark-shaped charm, used by Solomon Islanders, to ward off large sharks out of their nets (right)

Ivory

Sea spirit, with a shark-like head

Shark charm

Early 20th-century rattle for attracting sharks

Bark painting

Australian Aboriginal paintings often reveal what is inside an animal. This bark painting (left) shows the shark's liver with its two large lobes.

Shark tooth

Shark tooth

Shark weapons

Shark teeth were used by Pacific Islanders as weapons for cutting and slashing their opponents. Shark skin was used in other parts of the world to make sheaths for metal swords (below).

Early Hawaiian shark-tooth weapon

This shark-tooth glove from Kiribati protected a warrior's forearm

Sword used by the African Ashanti tribe

Shark-skin-covered sheath

Gold-plated handle

Shark attack

Most sharks are not dangerous and rarely attack humans. A person is more likely to be killed by a falling coconut than a shark. Every year, about 120 shark attacks are reported worldwide, with up to 10 of these being fatal. Take note of the warning signs and do not swim if the sea is murky, if you have cut yourself, or if bait has been put out for fish.

Tiger shark

Tiger sharks eat almost anything, including turtles, jellyfish, dolphins, and even people!

Wounded seal

Great white sharks often attack elephant seals by grabbing them from behind. Unlike people, these seals have plenty of energy-rich blubber.

Great white

Great whites have a reputation as bloodthirsty killers. They do attack people, but this may be because they mistake them for their natural prey.

Dummy attack

Wet suits do not protect against shark attacks, as this experiment with a dummy shows.

FATAL ATTACK

Most fatal shark attacks occur where people surf, swim, or scuba dive and where there are large sharks, like the great white, swimming close to shore.

Each year, around 92 people drown in the sea off Australia's coast ...

... while around eight people die from scuba diving accidents ...

... and less than one person dies from a shark attack.

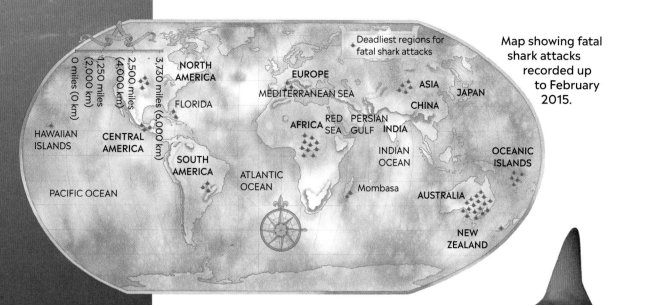

Map showing fatal shark attacks recorded up to February 2015.

Deadliest regions for fatal shark attacks

NORTH AMERICA
EUROPE
MEDITERRANEAN SEA
ASIA
JAPAN
CHINA
FLORIDA
AFRICA
RED SEA
PERSIAN GULF
INDIA
HAWAIIAN ISLANDS
CENTRAL AMERICA
INDIAN OCEAN
OCEANIC ISLANDS
SOUTH AMERICA
ATLANTIC OCEAN
Mombasa
AUSTRALIA
PACIFIC OCEAN
NEW ZEALAND

0 miles (0 km)
1,250 miles (2,000 km)
2,500 miles (4,000 km)
3,730 miles (6,000 km)

Bull shark

Bull sharks are one of the most dangerous sharks in the world, along with great whites and tiger sharks. The bull shark is one of the few sharks that swims in freshwater lakes and rivers.

Grey reef shark

When swimming normally, the back of a grey reef shark is gently curved and the pectoral fins are held straight. If threatened, the grey reef will arch its back and hold its pectoral fins downward.

👁 EYEWITNESS

Mistaken identity

A study by Australian researchers Nathan Hart and Dr. Laura Ryan found that because great white sharks cannot see well, other sharks, surfers, swimmers, and seals look the same to them from below the water surface. This is the first study to prove that most attacks by the great white shark on humans are a case of mistaken identity.

As many as

11 fatal shark attacks

were recorded in 2021.

Shark's-eye view

Sharks can mistake surfers for seals because they have similar shapes when seen from below.

49

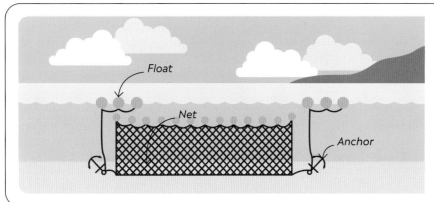

Mesh nets are used to trap sharks near popular beaches. The nets do not form a continuous barrier, so sharks may be caught on either side of the net. Other technologies include using drones for aerial surveillance of the coast, setting up shark listening stations that keep a record of tagged sharks swimming close to the beach, and wearing personal shark deterrent devices.

Sharks at **bay**

There is no simple way to protect people from sharks. Shark-proof enclosures can protect only small areas because they are expensive. In South Africa and Australia, nets are used along popular beaches to trap sharks, but they also catch harmless sharks, dolphins, rays, and turtles. Some countries use drumlines (baited lines with hooks). Other methods include magnetic, electrical, and chemical repellents. If a shark does become aggressive, punching or kicking its snout may put it off an attack.

Keeping sharks away

Tests conducted by Australian researchers Ry Kempster and Shaun Collin have shown that electric shark deterrent devices, such as Shar Shield, are effective. Devices, including wearab bracelets and special attachments for surfboards, generate an electric field that keep the sharks from coming closer.

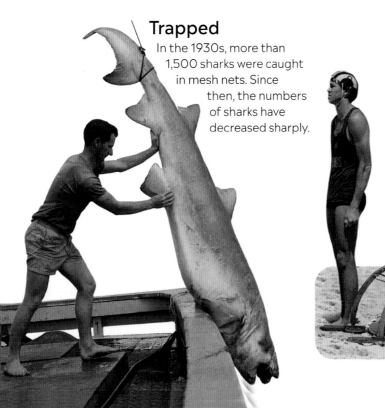

Trapped

In the 1930s, more than 1,500 sharks were caught in mesh nets. Since then, the numbers of sharks have decreased sharply.

In the bag

The US Navy found that sharks avoide people in inflatable bags because the could not see any limbs, sense any electrical signals, or smell blood or body wastes.

Life guards

If sharks are spotted near a beach, a shark alarm is sounded and swimmers must leave the water.

Chain wall

This wall of interlinked chains surrounding an Australian beach stops sharks from getting in. These walls are too costly to protect more than a few miles (km) of beach.

Protected beach

Of all the methods used to deter sharks, nets such as this one in Australia (above) seem to offer the best protection.

Invisible barrier

Here, an invisible electrical barrier is being tested. When the current is turned on, the shark turns back to avoid it.

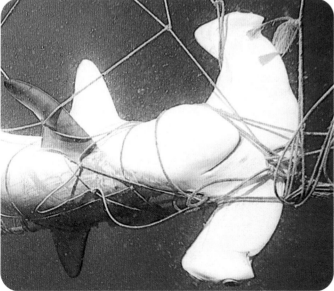

Death nets

Mesh nets, used to protect beaches, kill many sharks each year, like the great white (above) and hammerhead (left). Sharks caught in nets are not able to swim and suffocate because they cannot keep water flowing over their gills.

Shark repellent

If attacked, the Moses sole from the Red Sea releases a milky liquid from pores on its skin, causing the shark to spit it out.

Filming sharks

Diving with predatory sharks such as the great white (pp.28–31) can be dangerous, so underwater filmmakers and photographers use strong metal cages to protect themselves. With less dangerous species such as the blue shark (pp.56–57), divers sometimes wear chain-mail suits that prevent the shark's teeth from piercing the skin. When sharks are being filmed outside a cage, safety divers should also be present to look for sharks approaching from outside the filmmaker's field of vision.

Shining armor

Australian filmmakers Ron and Valerie Taylor are well known for their work on sharks. Valerie (pictured here) is testing the effectiveness of a chain-mail suit. The suits are heavy, so swimming is difficult. The blue shark is tempted to bite because the suit's sleeve contains pieces of fish. Butchers also use chain-mail gloves to protect their hands when slicing up meat.

1 Lowering the cage
Bait is thrown in the water to attract great whites. The metal cage is then lowered into the sea.

2 A great white approaches
It may be several days before a great white comes close to the cage, which is kept on the surface by floats.

Diving suit
In the 19th century, divers wore helmets and had air pumped down tubes from the surface.

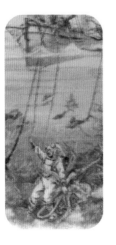

Diving with sharks

Australian conservationist Valerie Taylor has spent countless hours under the water with sharks. She started diving at a young age and, in the 1960s, Valerie and her husband Ron became the first people to film sharks in their natural habitat.

3 A view from inside the cage
Bait, like horse meat and tuna, attract the shark to the cage. The bars are close enough together to prevent the shark from biting the diver.

Many modern-day wetsuits are made of lightweight and bite-resistant materials.

Great white swims by
Divers can be shaken off their feet [as] the great white bumps into the cage. [Cl]ose-up views show just how big these [sh]arks are.

Filmmakers
Ron Taylor films a whitetip reef shark taking a bait, while a blue shark approaches the camera.

Studying sharks

To find out more about sharks, scientists attach electronic tags to their fins to monitor their movement and behavior. Great care is taken to keep sharks alive when they are caught for tagging and other studies. Certain types of sharks are placed in aquariums for observation (p.62).

Tracking by satellite

By tracking sharks, scientists have discovered that the great white swims long distances each year.

Acoustic tag

Tracking by signals

Acoustic tags transmit a unique signal that can be picked up by a receiver on a boat or attached to the seafloor. These tags allow tracking over a long period of time.

Aerial survey

Scientists use drones to study the behavior, movement, population, and social interactions of sharks in their natural habitat without interference. Drones are more cost-effective than using helicopters for gathering such data.

Recording sharks

Baited cameras can be deployed in oceans to observe and study sharks. These cameras have a caged bait attached to them, which attracts the sharks. Scientists can use such cameras to study the size, age, and population of the sharks.

Human interference

Marine scientist Adi Barash (pictured here with a panther electric ray) and her colleagues in Israel investigated reports of large numbers of sharks near coastal power stations in 2018. She found that human activities can change shark behavior. The sharks she studied stayed in the warm water discharged by the power stations for many days each year.

Lemon sharks

US scientist Dr. Samuel Gruber (1938–2019) studied lemon sharks for more than 10 years. Lemon sharks do not need to swim to breathe, so they can be kept still during observations. A substance is being injected into the shark (above) to show how fast it can grow.

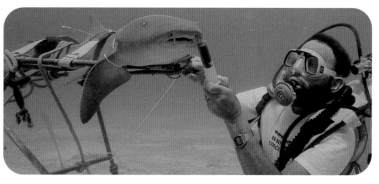

Water flow

Dr. Gruber checks the flow of water through this nurse shark's nose. Nurse sharks are normally docile, but they can give a nasty bite.

Tagging tigers

Scientists tag a small tiger shark (below left). A diver (below) pushes a tiger shark after tagging to keep water flowing over its gills.

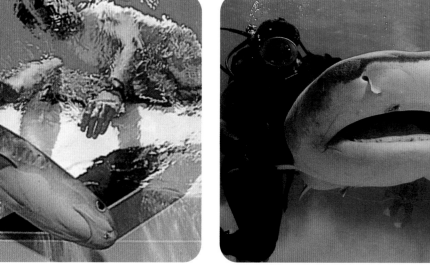

1 Tagging sharks

Like most sharks, blue sharks have an excellent sense of smell and are attracted to bait. Here, the shark hooks are baited with fresh mackerel, then the fishing lines are let out to depths of 40–59 ft (12–18 m).

2 Hooked

The shark takes the bait.

3 Reeling in

The shark is reeled in carefully.

Tagging sharks

Fishermen can help scientists find out where sharks go and how fast they grow by measuring, tagging, and releasing them. Today, most researchers use minimally invasive methods when tagging sharks. Tens of thousands of sharks have been tagged since the 1950s. Blue sharks are among the greatest ocean travelers. One tagged near New York was recaptured 16 months later off Brazil, 3,728 miles (6,000 km) away.

Satellite tags

Pop-up satellite archival tags (PSATs) send data via satellite so the shark doesn't have to be recaptured. These tags can be programmed to detach from the shark on a set date.

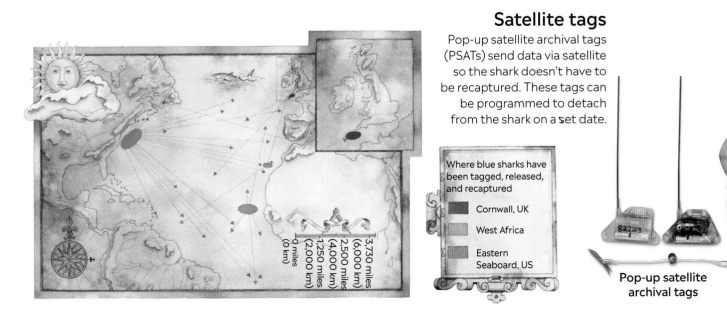

0 miles (0 km)
1,250 miles (2,000 km)
2,500 miles (4,000 km)
3,730 miles (6,000 km)

Where blue sharks have been tagged, released, and recaptured

Cornwall, UK

West Africa

Eastern Seaboard, US

82723

Pop-up satellite archival tags

5 Holding the shark down
The skipper holds the female shark down. He has to work quickly to insert the tag into her dorsal fin, as the shark cannot survive long out of the water. Buckets of saltwater are thrown onto the shark to keep her alive.

4 Thrashing shark
The thrashing shark is hauled in.

Blue flags show two sharks were released

326

6 Tagging the fin
The tag is made of strong metal that will not disintegrate in sea water and cause the plastic numbered tag to drop out. On the back is an address to where the tag can be sent if the shark is later recaptured.

7 Releasing
Holding the tail, the skipper gently lowers the shark back to the sea.

👁 EYEWITNESS

Floating laboratory
OCEARCH is a global organization that helps scientists collect data, which is widely shared. The team works on a ship that serves as a floating laboratory. A platform lifts a shark safely out of the water, allowing scientists to attach tags and take blood samples before it's released. The on-board laboratory allows the blood to be quickly analyzed, giving valuable data.

Overkill

People kill sharks for their meat, fins, skin, and liver oil, as well as for sport. But the biggest threat to sharks is overfishing and getting caught in nets laid for other fish, known as bycatch. Compared to bony fish, sharks take a long time to mature. If too many are killed, their numbers may never recover. Efforts are now being made to protect sharks by creating reserves, restricting numbers caught, and banning fishing.

Walls of death

Drift nets (top), some 50 ft (15 m) deep and many miles (km) long, are used to catch fish. The nets are so fine that sharks do not see them and become trapped in the mesh.

Cutting up sharks for mea

Bycatch

Many sharks are accidentally entangled in nets or caught on hooks meant for other fish. If they are unable to swim away, they can suffocate and die. Frequently, such bycatch numbers are not reported.

Fishing for food

In developing countries, people depend on shark meat for protein. In other countries, shark is a luxury food. It is important that shark fishing is controlled, as many species are at risk of becoming extinct.

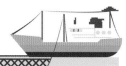

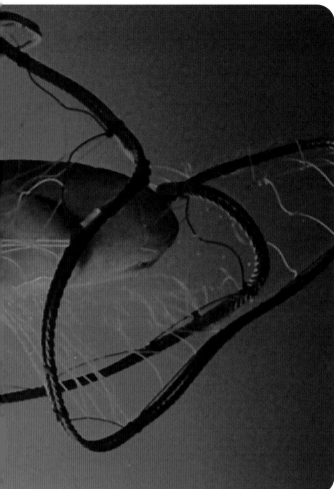

Working with fisherfolk
Dutch marine biologist Ayumi Kuramae has joined forces with the fisherfolk in the Dutch Caribbean to collect data and monitor the local shark populations. This has led to the establishment of the Yarari Sanctuary, which helps protect sharks.

Drying fins
Shark fin soup is a delicacy in the Far East. Because the fins can be dried, they are much easier to market than shark meat, which has to be sold quickly.

Shark fins drying

Fins of a shark are more valuable than other body parts.

Thrashed thresher
Thresher sharks are heavily fished in the Pacific and Indian Oceans. Landing a thresher can be dangerous, especially if they lash out with their tails.

Finning
These Japanese fishermen are cutting the fins off sharks caught in drift nets. They throw the rest of the shark back in the sea. Without fins, sharks are not able to swim properly and may be torn apart by other sharks.

Shark teeth

These pendants are made from the teeth of a great white shark.

Use and abuse

Over centuries, people have found a use for almost every part of a shark's body. The skin can be turned into leather, the teeth into jewelry, and the oil from the liver used in industry, medicines, and cosmetics. Today, sharks are killed mainly for food, and the demand for shark meat will probably continue. Human exploitation of sharks can cause a serious decline in numbers. If fewer people were to use products made from sharks, their future would be more secure. Otherwise, the effect on the natural balance in the oceans could prove to be disastrous.

Persian dagger

The sheath of this 19th-century Persian dagger is covered in lacquered ray skin.

Getting a grip

The shark skin on this sword handle gives a firm grip.

Rough shark skin

Curved ivory handle

Lacquered ray-skin-covered sheath

Rough ray skin under black cord

Samurai sword

This 19th-century sword covered in ray skin belonged to a Samurai warrior from Japan.

The shark skin on the handle of this British officer's sword has been dyed.

Box of happiness

Fine shark skin was used to cover this early 20th-century box from Korea. The leather is smooth because the denticles (p.7) have been highly polished, then lacquered and dyed dark green.

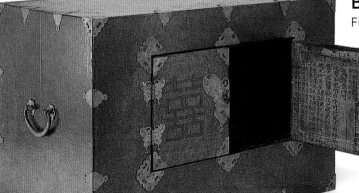

Shark and chips

Many sharks sold as food are misidentified or mislabeled as a another species or even other fish. Sadly, shark steaks are a fashionable delicacy in many restaurants worldwide.

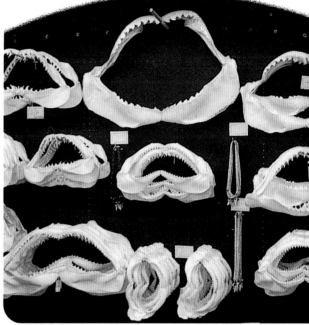

Jaws for sale

In the past, shark jaws were sold to tourists as souvenirs. The sale of great white shark jaws is now banned in many countries.

Headless corpse

This shark was killed for sport and its head was cut off so the jaws could be removed. Shark jaws are popular trophies among hunters.

Shark liver oil pills

Some people take shark liver oil pills to obtain vitamin A, but this vitamin can now be made artificially.

Shark liver oil pills

Two bowls and a can of shark fin soup

Polished, lacquered ray skin

Shark fin soup

The fibers in shark fins can be made into soup, which some people regard as a delicacy. The dried fins are soaked and repeatedly boiled to extract the fibers.

Shark remains

These two hammerheads (pp.42–43) were caught off the coast of Mexico. Their meat was probably used for food and their skin for leather goods, such as belts and wallets.

Skin care

Shark oil is used in costly skin creams. But other creams based on natural plant oils are just as effective.

Save the **shark!**

Sharks have a bad reputation as bloodthirsty killers. But only a few kinds of sharks are dangerous, and attacks on people are rare. Sharks are increasingly threatened by overfishing (pp.58–59). Some sharks, such as lemon sharks in Florida, also suffer because of the loss of mangrove swamps, which are important nurseries for their pups. People can learn more about sharks by visiting an aquarium. Good swimmers can learn to snorkel and scuba dive and may be lucky enough to see sharks in the sea.

Mad on sharks

This sculpture of a large shark on the roof of a house near Oxford, UK, shows just how much some people like sharks.

Making sketches of various sharks in an aquarium

Tanks for the view

Seeing sharks at close range is a great thrill. However, not all kinds of sharks can be kept in an aquarium. Smaller sharks such as smooth-hounds (pp.14–15) are the easiest, but many aquariums are introducing more unusual species. The Okinawa Churaumi Aquarium in Japan keeps whale sharks, and young great white sharks are sometimes kept in the Monterey Bay Aquarium in California.

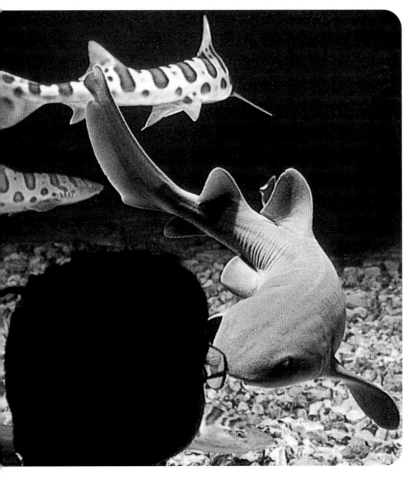

Learning about sharks

Join a conservation group that works to protect marine life. Look out for wildlife magazines and books about sharks. There are also interesting underwater programs on television that, unlike the scary *Jaws* movies, tell the real story about sharks.

Recording skate and ray egg cases

Certain kinds of ray and skate are also under threat. The UK-based charity the Shark Trust encourages people to record empty skate and ray egg cases that wash up on beaches. This may give clues as to the whereabouts of skate and ray nursery grounds.

Face to face with a shark (below left) and feeding time at the aquarium (below)

Sharks on file

Visiting aquariums, keeping a notebook, and drawing pictures of sharks are good ways of seeing how many different kinds of sharks there are. Compare the sharks' colors, skin patterns, and different body shapes. Write down the size, diet, natural habitat, and how the various sharks differ. With some effort, anyone can become more of an expert on sharks.

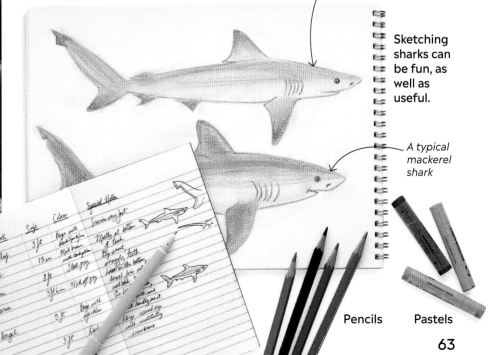

A sketch of a classic requiem shark, with its streamlined body

Sketching sharks can be fun, as well as useful.

A typical mackerel shark

Pencils   Pastels

Did you **know?**

AMAZING FACTS

Some Pacific islanders once worshipped sharks as gods, and therefore would never eat their meat.

Sharks have a large heart with four separate chambers.

Sharks often have very powerful jaws; some are capable of exerting 132 lb (60 kg) of pressure per tooth when they bite.

Boat builders in some parts of Africa rub the wood of a new vessel with hammerhead oil in the belief that it will ensure successful voyages.

Great white shark's tooth

A shark has an extremely stretchy, U-shaped stomach that can expand to accommodate an enormous meal that will last the animal several days.

A large part of a shark's brain is linked to its sense of smell; sharks can detect one part of scent in 10 billion parts of water.

Tiger sharks' teeth are strong enough to crunch through a turtle's bones and shell.

About 100 million sharks are killed each year due to fishing.

The spiral valve in a shark's intestine provides a relatively large surface area in a limited space. It slows digestion considerably, though, so a meal can take up to four days to digest.

Tiger shark's jaw

The Galapagos shark lives mainly around tropical reefs but may swim long distances between islands.

Galapagos shark

Shark skin is twice as durable as conventional leather.

Since they first appeared millions of years ago, sharks have probably changed less in evolutionary terms than any other vertebrate (back-boned animal).

In 17th-century France, shark brain was eaten to ease the pain of childbirth. It was also combined with white wine and taken for kidney stones.

On average, a shark can survive on 0.5–3 percent of its body weight per day.

Hawksbill turtle

Model of *cladoselache*, an ancient shark

Giving his work the title *The Physical Impossibility of Death in the Mind of Someone Living,* UK artist Damien Hirst exhibited an Australian tiger shark preserved in green embalming fluid inside a steel and glass tank in 1991.

Bite marks from cookiecutter sharks were discovered on the rubber coatin of listening devices on submarine belonging to the US Navy.

The meat of sharks (such as dogfish and even porbeagles) is still widely eaten, but that of the Greenland shark is inedible until left to rot. It is a delicacy in Iceland despite a strong flavor of ammonia.

Apart from people, a shark's greatest enemy is another shark; most sharks will happily eat any members of their own species. Orcas are also known to hunt great white sharks.

Upper tail (caudal) lobe

Gray-white color for camouflage

Thresher shark

Some species of shark can detect one-tenth of the light that an average person can see. Deep-water sharks have especially large eyes to help them penetrate the gloom.

Sharks are one of the most threatened groups of animals, with about 25 percent of shark species in danger of extinction.

Game fishermen often release sharks after they catch them.

Some kinds of sharks are fussy eaters; they sometimes take a sample bite out of their prey—or just sink their teeth in to get a taste—before they begin to feed properly. If they don't like the taste, they will spit out the bite and move on.

There are only a few records of sharks getting cancer. This has led to studies in the hope of finding anticancer substances in shark cartilage and other tissues. However, taking ground-up shark cartilage is unlikely to have any benefit.

One antishark device is a battery-operated machine designed to send out electrical impulses. This causes enough distress to approaching sharks to repel them. It can be fastened onto water craft or worn around the wrist or ankle.

Brain-to-weight ratios suggest that some kinds of sharks are of similar intelligence to birds and mammals. Sharks can be trained in exchange for food rewards; lemon sharks were trained to push a target with their snouts, and nurse sharks to bring rings.

Pectoral fin

Great white shark

A shark is able to detect an electrical field of only 100-millionth of a volt.

In order to feed, cookiecutter sharks travel from the bottom of the sea to the surface—a round trip of up to 4.4 miles (7 km).

Shark finning has been directly banned in at least 32 countries, with many others restricting shark fishing and finning.

When there's a large quantity of food available, sharks will gather around it in a feeding frenzy, during which they will bite anything that comes close, including each other.

Reef sharks feeding on surgeon fish

In some shark species, the female continues to produce eggs when she's pregnant, and the developing sharks eat them.

The hammerhead shark eats stingrays, swallowing them whole in spite of their poisonous spine.

Sharks prefer to prey on injured or diseased creatures than on strong ones that will fight back. Sharks will also eat dead fish. The great white sometimes feasts on whale carcasses.

The hammerhead's mouth is located under its head.

Hammerhead shark

Sharks can mistake reflections from metal or sparkly stones for fish scales. Avoid wearing jewelry when you're swimming where sharks have been seen!

Artificial skin from shark cartilage has been used to treat burns.

Did you **know?** (continued)

QUESTIONS AND ANSWERS

Pack of reef sharks hunting at night

Do sharks exist together in social relationships?

Species such as the white tip reef shark are known to hunt in groups. Great white sharks are sometimes found in pairs and small groups at feeding sites where larger sharks appear to dominate the smaller sharks.

Are sharks territorial?

Most sharks do not stay in the same place, but swim freely through the seas. Some species, such as gray reef sharks, establish a base and patrol it regularly. Similarly, whitetip sharks often stay in the same area for extended periods of time, but they are not known to defend their chosen territory.

Are sharks ever found in fresh water?

Most sharks live in the sea, but the bull shark, or Zambezi river shark, may swim into estuaries and up rivers and is sometimes found in lakes. As a result, it comes into closer contact with humans than other sharks. The bull shark is a large predator that sometimes attacks humans.

In what conditions is a shark attack on a person most likely to occur?

The majority of shark attacks occur where people like to paddle and swim. This is often during the summer months, when the water may be warmer. Attacks are most likely to take place in less than 6 ft 6 in (2 m) of calm water and within a comparatively short distance of the water's edge—about 35 ft (10 m). Particularly hazardous locations are protected inlets; channels where the water suddenly gets deeper; places where trash is dumped; and the immediate area around docks, quays, and wharfs, especially where people fish.

Bull shark or Zambezi river shark

How can swimmers lessen their chances of attack?

Sharks tend to attack people who are swimming on their own, so swimmers should always stay in a group. They should also avoid waters where seals, sea lions, or large schools of fish are often seen because sharks are attracted to these creatures. People who are bleeding, even from a small cut anywhere on their body, should remain on the beach because sharks can sense even the tiniest amount of blood in the water. They are also very sensitive to bodily waste, so it's dangerous to use the sea as a bathroom.

Seals can attract hungry sharks and so should be avoided by swimmers.

Is each different species of shark known by the same name in every part of the world?

The common names for sharks can vary widely. The bull shark has a great variety of names, likely because it is found in several different habitats. It is known as the Zambezi river shark, Lake Nicaragua shark, Ganges river shark, shovel-nose shark, slipway gray shark, square-nose shark, and Van Rooyen's shark.

Whale shark being filmed by a diver

OLD MAN OF THE SEA
Most sharks live for 20 to 30 years, but some reach 80. The Greenland shark is capable of surviving to 400, making it the longest-living vertebrate.

MINI MONSTER
One of the smallest species of shark is the dwarf lantern that grows to about 8 in (20 cm) long.

WHOPPING WHALE
The largest species of shark is the whale shark. It can measure at least 40 ft (12 m) long and weigh as much as 14.6 tons (13.2 metric tons).

GROWING PAINS
The fastest developers are large pelagic (open ocean) sharks, such as blue sharks; they can grow up to 12 in (30 cm) in a single year.

PLENTIFUL FOOD
Possibly the most common shark throughout the world is the spiny (piked) dogfish. It is also one of the more widely eaten species, so its numbers are declining.

HARD TO FIND
The megamouth shark, discovered in 1976, is one of the world's rarest species.

CHAMPION SWIMMER
The fastest-moving sharks are the blue and the mako. Blue sharks can reach speeds of up to 43 mph (69 kph), but only in short bursts. Mako sharks can swim at speeds of 50 mph (31 kph).

INTREPID TRAVELER
The most widely traveled species is the blue shark, which migrates up to 1,875 miles (3,000 km). A whale shark, tracked using a satellite tag, traveled 12,400 miles (20,000 km) in 841 days.

DANGER!
Amanzimtoti Beach in South Africa is one of the most dangerous beaches for shark attacks.

LONGEST TAIL
Thresher sharks have tails about as long as their bodies.

ANCIENT SURVIVOR
The frilled shark resembles primitive extinct sharks in that it has six pairs of gill slits.

Gill slit

Frilled shark

YAWNING HOLE
The jaws of *Carcharocles megalodon*, ancient ancestor of the great white, were 6 ft 6 in (1.8 m) across, while those of the largest recorded great white measure only 23 in (58 cm). Megalodon's teeth were also twice as big as those of the great white.

HOMEBODY
The least traveled shark is the nurse. It remains in the same section of reef for its entire life.

MURKY DEPTHS
The deepest level at which sharks have been sighted is around 13,000 ft (4,000 m).

Nurse shark

SHARK MANIA
Peter Benchley's book *Jaws* (1974) is one of the world's best-selling novels, and the first *Jaws* (1975) film is one of the world's top-grossing movies. However, due to the negative impact of his book on sharks, he later spent most of his life working for shark conservation.

PRIZE CATCH
Many records for the great white shark are exaggerated, such as one caught near Malta in 1992 that claimed to be 24 ft (7.10 m) long.

Find out more

Aquariums in many cities have impressive shark displays, and most can provide useful background information in the form of books, leaflets, photographs, lectures, and websites. Conservation organizations also provide information about sharks and encourage young people to get involved. The best way to learn about sharks is to see them in the wild. You can see some sharks from boats, including basking sharks and even great white sharks. Learning how to snorkel and scuba dive will also provide many opportunities to see sharks.

Behind bars

Most people observe sharks from the safety of a strong metal cage. The cages are never usually more than 10 ft (3 m) below the surface of the water.

An angel shark's eyes are on top of its head.

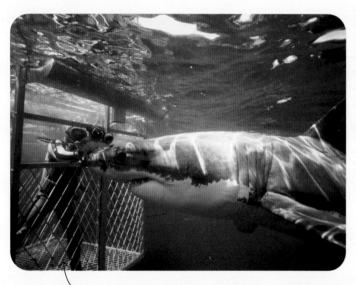

Shark cages are designed for protection against larger sharks—smaller species can slip through the gaps.

Visions of angels

Angel sharks are a popular aquarium attraction; however, they can be difficult to spot because they bury themselves in sand at the bottom of the tank.

Looking sharp

This historic necklace made from the teeth of a great white shark comes from New Zealand. Natural history museums often display similar objects.

Shark encounter

A clear observation tunnel at the Sydney Aquarium allows visitors to feel as if they are strolling along the ocean floor. Many aquariums exhibit large sharks, such as sand tigers and nurse sharks. Even whale sharks are on show in Japan and the US.

Fossil teeth one-quarter of their real sizes

Megalodon tooth

Great white tooth

USEFUL WEBSITES

- Official website of the Monterey Bay Aquarium
  www.montereybayaquarium.org
- Gives profiles of different species of sharks
  www.sharks-world.com
- UK-based conservation organization dedicated to protecting the world's sharks
  www.sharktrust.org
- The International Shark Attack File
  www.floridamuseum.ufl.edu/shark-attacks
- Official website of the Sydney Aquarium
  www.sydneyaquarium.com.au
- Official website of the London Aquarium
  www.visitsealife.com/london
- Useful website with good information on the biology of sharks and rays
  www.elasmo-research.org

Leopard shark

PLACES TO VISIT

WAIKIKI AQUARIUM, HAWAII

Shark enthusiasts will be particularly interested in:
- The Hunters on the Reef exhibit, which features zebra sharks, jacks, and giant groupers.

NATURAL HISTORY MUSEUM OF LOS ANGELES, CALIFORNIA

This museum contains more than 33 million specimens and related artifacts. Shark buffs will not want to miss:
- The rare megamouth shark, first of its species to be exhibited in a museum and the eleventh to be found since the shark's discovery in 1976.

MONTEREY BAY AQUARIUM, CALIFORNIA

This inspirational aquarium located on the coast of California features:
- A wealth of displays, talks, and sharks on show.
- A live web cam of sharks.

THE DEEP, HULL, UK

This wonder of modern architecture includes:
- A 33-foot (10-meter) deep tank containing nurse, sand tiger, and zebra sharks.

SEA LIFE SYDNEY AQUARIUM, AUSTRALIA

Located in Darling Harbour, this outstanding exhibition includes:
- A stunning open-ocean display where sharks can be observed at close range.
- More than 13,000 aquatic creatures in their natural environment.

SEA LIFE LONDON AQUARIUM, UK

This aquarium has a number of unusual displays, such as:
- Separate features on the Atlantic, Pacific, and Indian Oceans.
- Tours and shark feeds.

TWO OCEANS AQUARIUM, CAPE TOWN, SOUTH AFRICA

This aquarium is home to different kinds of sharks, including the ragged-tooth sharks.
- The *Save Our Seas Foundation Shark Exhibit* allows people to watch the sharks in their habitats and even interact with them.

Early coconut-shell rattle for attracting sharks from Samoa in the South Pacific

Glossary

Dogfish embryo

Ampullae of Lorenzini
Sensory pores on a shark's snout that help it pick up electrical signals from potential prey as it passes through the water. Scientists believe the ampullae of Lorenzini may also be involved in migration, acting as a kind of natural compass.

Anal fin A fin located on the underside of the body in some sharks.

Barbel Fleshy, sensitive feeler found near the mouth in some sharks. Barbels probe the sea bed to detect hidden food, and they may also help the shark smell and taste.

Barbel

Nurse shark

Buoyancy The ability to float. Sharks have an oily liver to help their buoyancy.

Cartilage Firm, gristly tissue that forms the skeleton of sharks. It is lighter and more flexible than bone.

Cartilaginous fish Fish that have a skeleton made of cartilage rather than bone. Cartilaginous fish include sharks, skates, rays, and chimaeras.

Caudal fin Tail fin. Within the various species, sharks have caudal fins of many different shapes and sizes.

Claspers Reproductive organs on the inner edge of a male shark's pelvic fins.

Cloaca Opening for the digestive, reproductive, and urinary tracts.

Copepod One of more than 4,500 species of tiny aquatic animals that make up plankton. Some of these attach themselves to sharks' fins and gills, feeding off their skin and blood.

Crustacea A group of hard-shelled aquatic creatures such as crab and shrimp, which provide food for some types of sharks.

Denticles Toothlike scales that form a protective layer on a shark's body. They are shaped differently according to species and where they appear on the body: the ones on the snout are rounded, while those on the back are more pointed. Dermal denticles are ridged, and they line up with the direction the shark is moving to minimize water resistance.

Dorsal Relating to an animal's back (opposite of VENTRAL).

Dorsal fin One of the fins located on the midline of a fish's back to stop it from rolling from side to side.

Denticles

Embryo An unborn animal that is developing inside its mother's womb or in an egg.

Feeding frenzy
The uncontrolled behavior of a group of sharks when there is blood or food in the water. During a feeding frenzy, sharks may attack one another.

Filter feeder An animal that feeds by straining plankton out of the water.

Fossil Remains of ancient plants or animals that have been preserved in sand or rock.

Gill raker
Comblike organ on the gill arch of some sharks. It strains plankton from the water taken into the shark's mouth.

Gills Breathing organs of fish through which oxygen is taken in. In sharks, the gills appear as a series of between five and seven slits behind the head.

Invertebrate Animal without a backbone or spinal column (opposite of VERTEBRATE).

Dorsal fin

Caudal (tail) fin

Black tip reef shark

Lateral line Row of cells that runs along each side of a shark's body and around its head. These organs are sensitive to changes in water pressure and can detect movement in the water—a great advantage when the sea is dark or murky.

Migration Regular movement of an animal population from one area to another and back again, often on a yearly basis.

Nictitating membrane A third, inner eyelid that moves across the surface of a shark's eye to clean and protect it.

Operculum Gill cover present in bony fish but not in sharks.

Oviparous Producing eggs that hatch outside the mother's body.

Nurse shark gills

Ovoviviparous Producing eggs that hatch inside the mother's body.

Parasite Animal or plant that lives on another organism and draws nutrients from it.

Pectoral fin One of a pair of fins located on the underside of the front section of a fish's body. Pectoral fins provide lift, help with steering, and act as brakes when necessary.

Pelvic fin One of a pair of fins located on the underside of the rear section of a fish's body. Smaller than pectoral fins, pelvic fins work with other fins to help with steering and act as stabilizers.

Plankton The mass of tiny plants and animals that float around in the sea and provide food for some shark species. Whale sharks, for example, live mostly on plankton.

A predatory bull shark hunting in the shallows

Predator An animal that hunts, eats, or kills other animals.

Prey An animal that is hunted, eaten, or killed by a predator.

Pup A baby shark.

School A large group of fish that swim closely together. Also called a shoal. A group of sharks is also called a shiver.

Seamount An underwater volcano or mountain.

Species A group of plants or animals that have common features.

Spiracles An extra pair of gill openings that supply oxygen to a shark's eyes and brain.

Spiral valve Corkscrew-shaped valve in the shark's intestine that helps with digestion. Some sharks have a scroll-shaped valve instead.

Tagging A method of identifying an individual animal, allowing it to be tracked and studied in the wild. Some tags record electronic information to help track them.

Tapetum lucidum A layer of cells at the back of the shark's eye. These cells reflect light, helping the shark see clearly in the dark.

Ventral Relating to the underside of the body (opposite of DORSAL).

Pectoral fin

Vertebrate Animal that has a backbone or spinal column (opposite of INVERTEBRATE).

Viviparous Producing young that remain in the mother's body until they are fully formed and ready to be born.

Horn shark

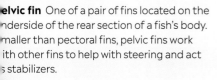

Tagging

Index

Acknowledgments

The publisher would like to thank the following people for their help with making the book: Alan Hills, John Williams, and Mike Row of the British Museum, Harry Taylor and Tim Parmenter of the Natural History Museum, Michael Dent, and Michael Pitts (China) for additional special photography; the staff of Sea Life Centres (UK), especially Robin James and Ed Speight (Weymouth) and Rod Haynes (Blackpool), David Bird (Poole Aquarium), and Ocean Park Aquarium (China), for providing specimens for photography and species information; the staff of the British Museum, Museum of Mankind, the Natural History Museum, especially Oliver Crimmen of the Fish Dept, the Marine Biological Association (UK), the Marine Conservation Society (UK), Sarah Powler of the Nature Conservation Bureau (UK), the Sydney Aquarium (Darling Harbour, Australia), John West of the Aust. Shark Attack File (Taronga Zoo, Australia), George Burgess of the International Shark Attack File (Florida Museum of Natural History, USA), Dr Peter Klimley (University of California, USA), and Rolf Williams for their research help; Djutja Djutja Munuygurr, Djapu artist, 1983/1984, tor bark painting; John Reynolds and the Ganesha (Cornwall) for the tagging sequence; Oliver Denton and Carly Nicolls as photographic models; Peter Bailey, Katie Davis (Australia), Muffy Dodson (China), Chris Howson, Earl Neish, Manisha Patel, and Helena Spiteri for their design and editorial assistance; Hazel Beynon for text editing; Vijay Kandwal for colour work; Priyanka Sharma-Saddi for the jacket; and Joanne Penning for proofreading and the index. **Maps:** Sallie Alane Reason. **Illustrations:** John Woodcock.

The publisher would like to thank the following for their kind permission to reproduce their photographs:
(Key: a=above; t=top; b=bottom/below; c=center; l=left; r=right)

Alamy Stock Photo: AF archive 60cla, Blickwinkel / McPHOTO / Bioquatic 8bl, Reinhard Dirscherl 32-33t, ZUMA Press Inc. 30cra, Nature Picture Library 34-35tr, Nature Picture Library 18tl, Louise murray 28tc, Martin Strmiska 1c, 42-43br. **Ayumi Kuramae:** Kevin Elis 59tr. **Adi Barash:** Adi Barash 54bc. **Ardea:** Mark Heiches 52cl; D. Parer & E. Parer-Cook 19tc; Peter Sleyn 8b, 30br; Ron & Val Taylor 7tr, 38bl, 40cl, 41tr, 52t, 52cr, 53tr, 53cr; Valerie Taylor 19bl, 51c, 51bl, 60tl; Wardene Weisser 8c. **BBC Natural History Unit:** Michael Pitts 64ca; Jeff Rotman 65tr, 66cla, 66bc, 67cla, 69c. **The British Museum/Museum of Mankind:** 46cl, 68bl, 69br. **Bridgeman:** The Prado (Madrid), *The Tooth Extractor* by Theodor Rombouts (1597-1637), 32cr. **Carlee Jackson:** Carlee Jackson 24cra;

Private Collection, *The Little Mermaid* by E. S. Hardy, 21tl. **Corbis:** Will Burgess/Reuters 50cr. **Capricorn Press Pty:** 56tl. **J. Allan Cash:** 27br, 50bc, 51tlb. **Bruce Coleman Ltd.:** 58br. **Neville Coleman Underwater Geographic Photo Agency:** 20tc, 44crb, 61cl. **Ben Cropp (Australia):** 50bl. **C. M. Dixon:** 47cr. **Dr. David Sims:** 2021 Marine Biological Association 34bc. **Dorling Kindersley:** Colin Keates / Natural History Museum 2tc, Dreamstime.com: Nataliia Velishchuk 48bc (DIVING), Dreamstime.com: Roman Vintonyak 2cla, 8clb; Colin Keates 25tr, 32br; Kim Taylor 21tl; Jerry Young 9cr, 42tr. **Richard Ellis** (USA): 17r. **Eric Le Feuvre** (USA): 20br. **Frank Lane Picture Agency:** 30crb. **Perry Gilbert** (USA): 51tr. **Peter Goadby** (Australia): 28t. **Getty Images:** Auscape 58clb, Portland Press Herald 54-55tc, Science & Society Picture Library 2br, 54cl, Fairfax Media 52bc, Ronald C. Modra 17cra, Len Deeley, photographer, underwater photographer 27t, The Washington Post 57br. **Julius Nielsen:** Greenland Institute of Natural Resources www.descna.com 44bl. **Greenpeace:** 58-59tc; 59br. **T. Britt Griswold:** 44b. **Tom Haight (USA):** 45t. **Edward S. Hodgson** (USA): 60lb, 61lb. **The Hulton Picture Company:** 34bl, 42cl. **Hunterian Museum, The University of Glasgow:** 13c. **The Image Bank** / Guido Alberto Rossi 30t. **F. Jack Jackson:** 49c. **Grant Johnson:** 54clb. **C. Scott Johnson** (USA): 50crb. **William MacQuitty International Collection:** 45bc. **Mary Evans Picture Library:** 36t, 38t, 52bl, 55br. **Macquarie University Lighthouse:** https://lighthouse.mq.edu.au 49crb; naturepl.com: naturepl.com: Brandon Cole 48-49c, Juergen Freund 54bl, Pete Oxford 56br, Mike Parry 31c. **National Museum of Natural History, Smithsonian Institution** (Washington, DC): Photo Chip Clark 13r. **NHPA:** Joe B. Blossom 23cr; John Shaw 23tl; ANT/Kelvin Aitken 48cr. **National Marine Fisheries Service:** H. Wes Pratt 54ct, 59bl; Greg Skomal 54bl; Charles Stillwell 23tc, 23tr. **Ocean Images:** Rosemary Chastney 28b, 29b, 29c, 54cl; Walt Clayton 15br, 48bl; Al Giddings 15cr, 45br, 48cl, 49br, 53bl; Charles Nicklin 29br; Doc White 20cl, 20bl. **Oceanwide Images:** Gary Bell 54cla. **Oxford Scientific Films:** Fred Bavendam 25tc, 39b: Jack Dermid 25cla; Max Gibbs 27cbr; Rudie Kuiter 43l; Godfrey Merlen 43cr; Peter Porks 35cr; Norbert Wu 45cr. **Planet Earth Pictures:** Richard Cook 57cr; Walter Deas 24bc, 39c, Daniel W Gotshol 30bl; Jack Johnson 51br; A. Kerstitch 21cr, 21bc, 21b; Ken Lucas 20tr, 24cr, 39tr, 42cla; Krov Menhuin 27bl; D. Murrel 32t; Doug Perrine 23br, 25cl, 26bcr, 54br, 55tr, 55cr, bc; Christian Petron 43bl; Flip Schulke 30tl, 55br; Marty Snyderman 20bl, 43tr, 54cr, 55tr; James P. Watt 32cla, 33cl; Marc Webber 30bl; Norbert Wu 26c, 49cr. **Marty Snyderman Productions:** clb.

Courtesy of Sea Life Centres (UK): 62bl. **The Shark Trust:** 63tr. **Courtesy of Sydney Aquarium** (Darling Harbour, Australia): 62br. **Werner Forman Archive** / Museum of Mankind: 47cl. **Courtesy of Wilkinson Sword:** 60cl. **Rolf Williams:** 16tl, 18cr (in block of six), 61tr.

All other images © Dorling Kindersley.
For further information see: **www.dkimages.com**

Map update references

30-31 Gubili, C., Duffy, C., Cliff, G., Wintner, S., Shivji, M. S., Chapman, D. D., et al. (2012). "Application of molecular genetics for conservation of the great white shark, Carcharodon carcharias, L. 1758," in Global Perspectives on the Biology and Life History of the White Shark, ed. M. L. Domeier (Boca Raton, FL: CRC Press), 357-380. (Great White Shark)

32-33 Pierce, S. J. & Norman, B. 2016. Rhincodon typus. The IUCN Red List of Threatened Species 2016: e. T19488A2365291. https://dx.doi.org/10.2305/IUCN. UK.2016-1.RLTS.T19488A2365291.en. Accessed on March 16, 2022. (Whale Shark)

34-35 Rigby, C. L., Barreto, R., Carlson, J., Fernando, D., Fordham, S., Francis, M. P., Herman, K., Jabado, R. W., Liu, K. M., Marshall, A., Romanov, E. & Kyne, P. M. 2021. Cetorhinus maximus (amended version of 2019 assessment). The IUCN Red List of Threatened Species 2021: e.T4292A194720007. https://dx.doi.org/10.2305/IUCN.UK.2021-1.RLTS. T4292A194720078.en. Accessed on March 16, 2022. (Basking Shark)

36-37 IUCN. 2021. The IUCN Red List of Threatened Species. Version 2021-3. https://www.iucnredlist.org. (Angel Sharks)

42-43 Habitat of Hammerheads © www.SharkSider.com

44-45 Kyne, P. M. 2018. Isistius brasiliensis. The IUCN Red List of Threatened Species 2018: e.T41830A2956761. https://dx. doi.org/10.2305/IUCN.UK.2018-2.RLTS.T41830A2956761.en. Accessed on March 16, 2022. (Cookiecutter Shark) Kyne, P. M., Gerber, L. & Sherrill-Mix, S. A. 2015. Isistius plutodus. The IUCN Red List of Threatened Species 2015: e. T60212A3093223. https://dx.doi.org/10.2305/IUCN. UK.2015-4.RLTS.T60212A3093223.en. Accessed on March 16, 2022. (Largetooth Cookiecutter Shark)

48-49 Statista: Data from: The World's Deadliest Regions for Shark Attacks https://www.statista.com/chart/3590/the-worlds-deadliest-regions-for-shark-attacks/ (Shark Attacks)